The Art of Seduction

The guide to becoming self-confident goodness and a master of seduction

Victoria Onica

Victoria Onica

THE ART OF SEDUCTION

"The guide to becoming self-confident
goodness and a master of seduction"

ISBN: 9798847887298

Cover design by: Natalia Fostica

Table of Contents

INTRODUCTION

Mention "seduction," and you have most people's immediate and undivided attention. Everybody is interested in learning more about how to seduce. Whether they are starting in the dating game or they've been married for 25 years and are longing to put some of the sparks back into their relationship.

This book will tell you everything you need to know about becoming the sizzling seductress or seducer you've always wanted to be. And, as I hope you will become abundantly clear while you're reading when I talk about seduction, I am not talking about the archaic, manipulative act with which many of us have come to associate the word.

The seduction you'll learn about in this book is the art of enticing your partner and creating an exquisitely pleasurable experience for both of you.

It's far more appropriate to think of seduction as a process rather than an act. And it is a process you must undertake with the purest intentions. If there's one theme that will show up again and again in this book, it is that the most powerful element in any seduction is the intent of the seducer.

In order for you to be able to seduce another person in a positive way, your desires must be grounded in a concern for the well-being of both, you and your partner.

- So who is this book for?
- For everybody!

Never make the mistake of thinking that seduction is only for the young and starry-eyed, or for people in the beginning stages of a relationship.

Two other points I hope to make clear in this book are that, seduction is for everyone and seduction is forever.

If some of the chapters seem more focused on people who are going out and seducing somebody for the first time, this is only because I know how intimidating that "first time" with someone can be— no matter how experienced you are.

Even so, nearly all of the advice in this book can be applied to bringing elements of seductiveness into a long-term relationship as well. To me, the best relationships are those in which both parties keep the seduction alive continuously.

And if you don't think perpetual seduction is possible…well, just read this book!

In the final analysis, seduction is a true art form.

Some people believe that artists are born rather than made, and others believe that anyone who has the benefit of sufficient training in technique can become an artist. I firmly believe the latter is true. But, of course, just as with any other art form, seduction is about more than technique.

A genuinely delicious seduction is a combination of feelings, intentions, and techniques, with the end result truly being greater than the sum of its parts. If this sounds hopelessly abstract, it's not. Being seductive is really quite simple if you follow the concrete guidelines in this book.

CHAPTER 1

Redefining seduction

Seduction—what a titillating topic. The very word holds a promise of tantalizing pleasures, sensual indulgence, or, perhaps, forbidden delights. If you're like most of today's women and men, however, you're not hungering for forbidden fruit. You simply want a pragmatic, honest, and mutually pleasurable path to enticing a lover.

We're going to set the stage for your transformation into a modern-day seductress or seducer. After learning a new definition of seduction—as it befits the new era we're approaching—you'll learn how to take a proactive approach to your love life by setting goals.

You'll discover the elements of seductiveness—all those facets of you that make up the alluring whole—and you'll learn how you can enhance them in order to create your captivating new self.

So…let the magic begin!

You want to be seductive. Hmmm…where to begin? Just by virtue of having the desire to be so, you're already on the path to seductiveness. And you've definitely come to the right book.

Before we begin the how-to, though, I want to make sure we're all in agreement about what seduction means. There are easy as many negative as positive connotations for this word. For example, seduction can imply coercion and abuse of power. Over the years, the news media has assailed us with various high-profile cases, though in some instances, it was difficult to tell just who was seducing whom.

On the other hand, we have hopelessly sweet and romantic images of seduction, many of which are fictional (the movie Don Juan de Marco comes to mind, for example). There are, however, countless true-life cases in which people are seduced in a delightful manner by someone who really has their best interests in mind. This cases don't make the headlines.

The point is that there is bad seduction and good seduction—or, you might say, malicious and delicious seduction. Too often in the past, seduction has implied a harmful variety. With this in mind, I think it's time for the entire concept of seduction to get an overhaul.

Our aim here is to define or redefine seduction for real life (as opposed to reel life). We're going to look at seduction as a way to:

- Be alluring
- Be charismatic
- Be enticing

I want to make it clear that the focus of this book is the new seduction—seduction for the new millennium if you will. For many of us, this new millennium that everyone's talking about holds the promise of being a more joyous, happy time, a time when people will become more conscious of, and motivated toward, a general state of well-being.

It follows that the shift in emphasis of seduction would be toward actions that would have a positive effect on a person's spirit and life in general.

The seduction we're going to talk about in this book is a seduction that goes beyond purely selfish intent and results in the benefit of all involved.

A thousand years of good intent

English is a flexible language. As linguists and other scholars continue to remind us, we have always changed the meanings of words according to time, place, and circumstance.

Seduction is certainly one of those words whose meaning has changed with the times. Originally, to seduce someone or to be seductively meant to do something to the person or to entice a person to do something that was generally not in his or her best interest.

Over the years, however, the definition has expanded to include actions taken to win over or attract another person. The context may or may not be sexual, and the results may be beneficial or harmful. In just a little while, we'll explore examples of the varieties of seduction—nonsexual and sexual, beneficial and hurtful.

How do you tell the "good" from the "bad"?

What's the difference between the archaic, negative seduction and the new, enlightened sort of seduction we'll be exploring in this book. The distinction lies in two factors:

1. **The intent or purpose:** You can judge whether your actions represent the new seduction or the old based on your motives. Are you just after a momentary thrill, with no regard for the welfare of the person you're seducing (or for how you'll feel about yourself when it's all over)? Or do you truly want to create a pleasurable experience for both of you?

2. **The results:** For better or worse, the effects of seduction almost always outlast "the act." The ultimate results are as significant as the intent (and we all know what they say about the road to hell). Consider the residuals of your act: Will it leave one or both of you with feelings of guilt or regret or with smiles on your faces?

If your intent is benevolent and your actions bring no harm to that person—or to yourself—then it's safe to say you were practicing the "new" seduction. Just to make sure we're clear on the distinctions between the various types of seduction, we'll look at a few examples.

Nonsexual seduction: The good, the bad, and the downright ugly.

Seduction comes in many forms, it isn't always about sex. In fact, sometimes it isn't even about you and another person.

Something to which we can all relate: Food.

Let's say you get hold of a big red apple and it looks so fresh that you just know it's going to be crisp and juicy and sweet. Your mouth begins watering at the mere thought of that first bite. That apple is calling to you—yes, seducing you—until you can't resist anymore. You close your eyes, almost as if in prayer, open your mouth wide, and take that first, tantalizing bite.

Exactly as you had imagined, it has just the right crunch, and it is bursting with sweet juiciness. When you separate yourself from the rapture of that first taste, your intellectual side tells you that it's nutritious—certainly not a symbol of original sin, but simply a piece of delicious fruit.

As you eat it, your body feels better, and you seem to have more energy—you are filled with a sense of having been both nourished and delighted. There are no regrets, your body and your mind seem to smile in unison.

On the other hand, imagine that you're on a diet, and you're being tempted by a piece of pecan pie. That pie calls to you and sings to you. Though you know the pie is full of fat, calories, and artery-clogging cholesterol, its sweetness has an almost hypnotic appeal. Throwing caution and moderation to the wind, you eat the pie.

After all, you've been depriving yourself for weeks now. But somehow, when you're finished, you don't feel rewarded. You immediately feel heavy and guilt-ridden. You feel bad about yourself, and your self-image has taken a minor nosedive.

For the purpose of this example, then, we can say the act of eating the pie represents bad seduction, whereas eating the apple represents good seduction.

Seducers on two legs

In the food examples, we just listed, there really wasn't the factor of intent or purpose—at least not from the objects that seduced us. Apples and slices of pecan pie are not sentient beings, but you could, however, consider these examples to be cases of self-seduction, in which case the pie incident would constitute self-sabotage.

Now, let's look at some examples involving other people. Imagine you're at a party, and a woman you know comes up to you and says, "Michael, you're so good with children. You're so funny. Kids think you're just like a clown.

I would just love to dress up for you as a clown on Christmas Eve and spend a couple of hours in the burn section of the Children's Hospital. Just giving the kids gifts and talking to them...you know, generally lifting their spirits."

Almost without your realizing it, she seduces you into taking time out of your frantic holiday schedule to visit the hospital. It's easy to understand why. The person making the request is someone who likes you and holds you in high esteem, and you feel the same about her. She has appealed to your higher self, enmeshing you in the holiday spirit and the natural glow that comes from doing good deeds.

Afterward, of course, you feel wonderful. You think of how fortunate you are to be healthy, and you're glad you brought some joy into these children's lives. You even promised yourself: "This is something that I will do every year from now on, because I do not only bring joy to the kids, it made me feel good."

Did the person who originally seduce you into going to the hospital and becoming a clown practice negative or positive seduction? Obviously, this is a case of a positive one.

Picture yourself at another party. A woman you know who's a stockbroker comes up to you and says, "Michael, I have the greatest deal for you. I have some inside information, no one else has about a stock that's about to split. You're going to make so much money if you buy it.

Just think how great you'd look in that new Porsche you've been wanting." Glossing over that phrase "inside information," you let yourself be talked into buying the stock.

Why? This woman has appealed to your greedy side and your vanity. You want to make money, and besides, you really like the broker's implication that you would be more attractive with an expensive new car. So you purchase the stock—and then it doesn't split, after all. In the end, you lose a lot of money.

The woman did, indeed, seduce you, but not in a good way, and you ended up feeling used. She made a huge commission, and what did you get? Nothing, but a big dose of what avarice will do to you.

That is the negative form of seduction.

Sexual seduction: the sublime and the squalid

For most of us, the word "seduction" has sexual connotations above all else. After all, that's why you're reading this book, isn't it? Sexual energy is a powerful force, and when the factor of seduction is added, it can either move your soul or shatter you to your very core. Again, it all depends on how it is used—the intent and purpose and the results.

Delicious seduction: a little slice of heaven

Imagine that you're coming home from a hard day at work, and you haven't had a very good day with the boss. You're cranky and tired. As you pull into the driveway, you see your husband's car. He's home early.

That's curious, he's not usually home before you. Half suspicious, half worried, you fumble for your keys and push open the front door—only to look across the foyer to the stairs, where you see a rose petal on each step, beckoning you up the stairway.

What's this? You wonder. Following the trail of rose petals, you are led into the bathroom, where you see a tiny envelope with your name on it. You open the envelope and read the note inside.

The note says: "My Love, the bubble bath is drawn for you. I hope it's the right temperature. I put in the rose-scented bath salts you like so much. On the vanity, you will find one champagne glass and a chilled bottle in the bucket next to the tub. Please pours yourself a glass, slip into the tub, and just let the day fade away. I Love You."

You get into the tub, simply delighted. Your husband has never done anything like this before. You lie there in the gentle caress of the bubbles, sipping the champagne, and you begin to drift off and actually forget about how bad your day was.

Then you get out and find a brand-new, big, fluffy bath towel waiting there with another note pinned to it.

The note says: "This towel was made for one purpose: to pamper the most beautiful body that I have ever seen. After you are finished drying off, please come into the bedroom."

The softness of the towel delights you as you dry your body. You find that you're laughing now, your frustration washed away, replaced by the feeling that you are beautiful.

You go into the bedroom and find another note: "Lie down on the bed and put on this mask. Listen to the music I've selected on the stereo, and just relax. In a few moments, I'll come in and give you a massage. My hope is that my hands will speak clearly, and tell you just how much I adore you."

You put the mask on and lie down, completely lost in the sense of sheer delight. The music begins softly, barely audible, then rises just loud enough for you to recognize and follow the melody. Strains of "Winter" from Vivaldi's Four Seasons begin to weave their unique spell.

God, how long have you loved this piece? Your reverie is only slightly interrupted by the feel of warm oil, gently pressed into your skin by two strong, sensitive hands—hands that you know and that know you so very well.

The touch is soft but masculine upon your neck and shoulders, moving down your body, sweetly kneading away what little tension remains in your now supple flesh. He just keeps on, working for those hands down the length of your body, all the way down to your toes. He isn't saying anything to you, yet you hear him well.

As you start to drift off, completely relaxed, you feel the slight tickle of a feather upon your skin, grazing lightly across your breasts and sending tingles, so familiar, yet brand new, through your body. Without even fully awakening, you reach out, drawing this wondrous man close to you, and the two of you make love passionately.

And yes, my dear, you have just been delightfully and completely seduced.

Think about this scene (how can you not?). Was this a sweet seduction for the new millennium—delicious seduction, in other words—or an example of the old, "evil," malicious seduction?

Consider the intent. Your husband went to some trouble to put this entire scenario together, and he did this out of adoration for you. Think of the results. During the next few days, you find your mind drifting back to that wonderful afternoon, thinking every day about how loved you feel, and appreciating all of the work and thought that went into giving you such a delightful experience.

This seduction left nothing in its wake but warm, tender emotions, increased feelings of self-worth, and the sense that the two of you are closer to each other than ever before.

Obviously, this was an example of delicious seduction.

Malicious seduction: devil on a blue bike

Now, let's take a look at another scenario. It's late at night, and you go to a bar. You start dancing with a pretty good-looking guy in a motorcycle jacket. He's whispering something in your ear that you can't quite understand, and as you drink and dance and drink some more, things begin to get very sexy. Before you know it, it's getting late, but he keeps buying you drinks, and pretty soon, your mind is a little foggy.

Then he invites you to take a ride on his motorcycle and maybe come over to his place. That doesn't sound like such a great idea, mainly because you're in a committed relationship with a terrific boyfriend who's out of town and because this leather-clad man is a complete stranger.

But your new friend keeps up the pressure until you finally give in and go with him. When you get to his house, he opens up a bottle, and you have more to drink. Next thing you know, you're having some very rough sex.

Afterward, your head spinning from the booze, you fall asleep.

The next morning, you awaken early and find yourself next to someone you don't know at all, who is not nearly as sexy as he was the night before. He has a growth of beard on his face, and his breath reeks of stale beer.

You look around and really observe the way he lives, the place that you've put yourself in. To say that he's not very tidy would be an understatement, and you find that you want more than anything in the world, just to be away—from him, from his filthy place, and, sadly, from yourself most of all. Your self-worth is about as low as it's ever been, and you feel very ashamed that you have been unfaithful to.

Right now, you're experiencing what is known as "coyote love." A coyote, caught in a trap, will literally gnaw its own leg off to escape, and, at this moment, you would almost rather do the same thing than wake this guy up and ask him to drive you home.

This scenario, too, was a seduction, but what type was it? Was it delicious or malicious? The best way to tell is to ask yourself how you feel. Your self-worth is down, you don't even want to speak to this person, and God knows what horrible disease you might now carry. This clearly falls into the category of bad seduction.

There's no such thing as an one-night stand: seduction has lasting effects

When you engage in good seduction, you must have no harmful intent in mind for the person you're seducing. On the contrary, you must wish for this individual as much pleasure, both short and long term, as you desire for yourself.

As we just saw in the example above, a bad seduction inevitably has a toxic outcome.

If your intent is clearly focused on your own selfish need, oblivious to the well-being of your partner, the outcome will always be less than joyous. After you've been on the receiving end of such a toxic seduction, you feel like you've been drained, as if the life force has just been sucked out of you. You're left feeling tired and not very pleased with who you are.

On the other hand, if you've been seduced by someone who holds your own well-being high on their priority list, life somehow seems better for you. And if you're the kind of sweet seducer who holds the pleasure and well-being of your partner as dearly as your own, the rewards you will reap go beyond those of a carnal nature.

In either case, seduction has effects that last long past the act itself. That's why it's always important to consider not just the intent but the results.

Ingredients to cast a seductive spell

What exactly does this magical substance consist of? It's not any single element or quality. It's certainly not anything that you can drape over yourself before walking out the door to greet the world. Rather, charisma is the essence of the person, the sum of all the person's other qualities and characteristics—and as such, it takes on its own energy.

This is one instance in which the whole is truly greater than the sum of its parts. It's much like a precious stone, which shines clearly with the reflected light of its many facets. Should one or more of the facets be flawed, the stone fails to shine and its value is diminished. However, with all facets polished to perfection, the gem exudes a light and splendor that is a source of awe and wonderment.

So, what are the magical ingredients of seductiveness?

- **A pinch of physical attraction**: The first important element is physical body and appearance. Physical presence is both an outgrowth of a person's attitude toward him or herself and a factor in the shaping of that attitude. Obviously, a person tends to be happier and, thus, more attractive if he or she is in good health. Grooming and hygiene are certainly factors in a pleasing physical appearance as well. And to a lesser, but still significant, extent, what a person wears can also enhance his or her self-image if the cut and fabrics are sensual and signal approachability. Approachability is a key word here. A truly seductive person looks warm and real and touchable, unlike some of the stunning beauties or hunks we often see on TV and in the movies. We'll learn about physical attraction in Chapter 3.

- **A dash of intellectual magnetism:** Another element of a person's essence is the mind. To be truly seductive, a person must be stimulating on an intellectual level. After all, it has been rightfully said that our primary erogenous zones are in our minds. What makes a person interesting? In general, a truly interesting person is one who has a keen sense of curiosity and is able to communicate that interest. This person expresses interest in you in a way that lets you know there are things he or she wants to learn from you, as well as teach you. Such a person has a hunger for knowledge about the surrounding world and about the person he or she is with.

- **A touch of emotional seductiveness**: No less crucial than any of the other elements is the person's emotional being. By emotional being, we mean the ability to feel compassion, to open him- or herself to feel for you, to have empathy with your plight or even the plight of someone he or she has never met, half a world away.

- **An emotionally attractive person experiences joy merely by touching or being touched by you in a safe and tender way**. And that is extraordinarily seductive. In Chapter 5, we'll discuss emotional seductiveness.

- **Mix well, and you have...spirit.** Finally, we come to the person's spirit, or essence—and we're right back where we started. Spirit (to return to our original metaphor) is truly the luminescence of the precious gem, emanating from its many facets and shining its light out into the world. This essence includes how a person looks, thinks, and how he or she emotes, but it also includes factors that are less immediately discernible. Among these are a person's self-confidence and sense of self-worth, and intent toward others.

- **The good news is that by focusing on your own individual "elements"**—the physical, intellectual, and emotional aspects that make up your essence—you can be seductive and charismatic yourself. Before we get into these elements of seductiveness, however, we need to talk about goal setting.

CHAPTER 2

Goal Setting: The proactive approach to seduction

This chapter is about goal setting—deciding exactly what you want and beginning the process of getting it. If you're an incurable romantic, you may be wondering why we're talking about goal setting at all in a book about seduction. Perhaps you think any mention of goals in this context sounds too much like a business and not enough like pleasure.

Maybe you believe that goal setting will rob seduction of its mystery and magic. Relax! That's not the intent here at all.

Being a romantic myself, I'm a great fan of mystery and magic—but I am also a firm believer in taking a proactive approach in all areas of life. In truth, goal setting is every bit as valid in your personal life as in your business dealings.

Think of it this way: Most of us have experienced romances that ended in disaster or perhaps just in disappointment. And why did this happen? More than likely, it was because we set out blindly, with no idea of what we truly wanted and needed. We didn't have any goals. So we just let things happen.

Whose life is it, anyway?

You might not have thought about it, but you have already begun the process of setting goals. After all, you've decided you want to attract people, haven't you? That, in and of itself, is a goal. What have you done to achieve this goal? Well, you bought this book, that's a good first step.

Now you're already on your way to becoming seductive.

In making the decision to become seductive, what you have really decided to do is to re-create yourself, which is not nearly as daunting as it may sound at first. After all, I'm not talking about turning yourself into something you're not. That would not only be destructive, but it would also be impossible.

Instead, I am talking about becoming aware of and refining your dreams about yourself and, through a focused, proactive effort, bringing those dreams to life.

Nobody else can do it for you, and it is going to take some effort on your part. The result, however, will be well worth it. You can and will transform yourself into the most desirable person you can be, and the people around you will most certainly sit up and take notice. To paraphrase a line from a popular movement a few years back, "If you build it, they will come."

It's your life, and you can make it as glorious as you want it to be.

Maybe she/he's born with it…but probably not.

Some people just seem to be naturally seductive. In truth, however, very few people are born knowing how to be a great seductress or seducer. A look at some classic examples of alluring seductresses and irresistible playboys illustrates the point that seductive people are not born but made (in more ways than one!).

23

Classic seductresses: Geishas and Courtesans

Arthur Golden's fascinating and well-researched novel Memoirs of a Geisha describes in delicious detail the life, training, and mindset of a Geisha. A Geisha is trained from her childhood to attract, please, and entertain men, particularly wealthy businessmen.

Although we may look upon it as servitude, becoming a Geisha was, and is, considered a very noble and revered calling in Japan. Girls chosen for this training are selected not just for their physical beauty but also for their ability and motivation to learn the required skills.

Training begins early with a highly organized apprenticeship. The young girl receives extensive instruction in skills and traits valued by men of power: music, the arts, voice, make-up, and hair. She learns to converse about everything from history to current events to the gossip of the day.

Her objective is to become ever more desirable, more alluring, and more intoxicating to the men she will entertain.

Indeed, the ability of the Geisha to absolutely enthrall her charges is legendary. And the book Memoirs of a Geisha is an extraordinary story of how an ordinary girl transforms herself into an incredible seductress.

A similar transformation takes place in a movie called Dangerous Beauty. This is a splendid (though admittedly somewhat idyllic) presentation of the life of a courtesan.

The movie shows how a common girl is transformed into a courtesan and becomes so phenomenally seductive that the citizens of an entire city are ready to lay down their lives for her.

In Europe in the 16th and 17th centuries, a courtesan was a woman who was thoroughly and painstakingly trained in all aspects of seduction and allure: education, wit, entertainment, and beauty.

Far from being a common prostitute, the courtesan was placed in a position of respect and power to a degree far beyond that of her female contemporaries.

She frequently stood beside her man of the moment at important social and political functions. This position was not bestowed haphazardly. The courtesan had to learn well the skills that would inspire others to look upon her with respect.

In the examples above, neither the Geisha nor the courtesan was born knowing the ropes. They learned to become seductive. And the lesson for us modern, enlightened women are that we, too, can transform ourselves into enthralling creatures.

Naturally, I am not suggesting that you have to become a Geisha or a courtesan in order to be seductive. However, if the women of these more repressive societies could use their allure to rise above many of the limitations placed upon them, imagine how empowered an independent, modern woman could become if armed with the basic talents and wisdom of courtesans and Geishas.

The good news is that, unlike the Geisha and the courtesan, the woman of today don't need to spend years in training to become seductive. Make the decision, apply the process to yourself, and you'll see positive results in only a few months.

Bond, James Bond

A seductive man with whom we are all familiar is the character of 007, James Bond. Granted, Bond is fictional, but I cite him because, fictional or not, he is a reflection of our culture's ideals of masculine allure.

Just what is it about this character that makes him so appealing to women? Is it his looks? That's only part of the story. While the actors who have played the British secret agent in many Bond movies have all been attractive, their attractiveness was not based solely on the actors' physical appearance.

The truth is, James Bond wouldn't be nearly as sexy if he didn't know all of the things he knows. He comes across as being completely comfortable in circumstances that most of us will never face, and his repertoire of knowledge includes areas that, while exciting, are completely foreign to most people.

After all, he's a spy, he's an incredible marksman with any kind of weapon, he can drive a race car, and he knows martial arts. It is obvious that he's in great physical condition, as he routinely performs acts that would leave the average man, at best, sore for weeks and, at worst, in the hospital or dead. With all those qualities at his disposal, it's almost inconsequential that he's good-looking.

The point is that, the things that make James Bond so attractive are virtually all things that he has learned, as opposed to naturally inborn qualities.

What about You?

All of this people who were so phenomenally attractive started off as ordinary people. Yet, by acquiring skills and knowledge, which they applied to their lives, they transformed themselves into objects of near-worship.

It isn't stretching the truth at all to tell you that you, too, are capable of transforming yourself into an alluring, desirable person. It takes some work, and it definitely takes a real commitment, but you can do it. You simply have to:

1. Realize that wherever you are right now is the perfect place to start.
2. Determine what you have to work with.
3. Compare what you are with what you would like to be.
4. Figure out the straightest path between the two.

Short-term goals: the first person you must seduce is yourself

Becoming seductive is just like any other desire you may have.

You must define the desire before you can hope to realize it.

Therefore, the first step toward becoming more seductive is to establish a picture in your mind of just what a seductive "you" would look like, sound like, feel like, and even smell like. In short, you need to determine just how a sexy "you" would appear in your own mind.

As I've said before, the image you hold of yourself is the one that others around you are most likely to perceive. Thus, the focus of this short-term goal is really on seducing yourself.

That's the first step in seducing someone else.

Your short-term goal, then, is to make a commitment to become the sexiest, most alluring, most charismatic being you possibly can. Here's how to do it:

- **State your goal to yourself.** "I want to become a seductress," or "I want to become a seducer." Don't worry about concrete definitions of what that means, for now, it is important only that you acknowledge that you want to achieve something.
- **Write down your goal.** You'd be surprised what a difference that will make in turning your future goal into a reality.
- **Decide on a period in which to reach your goal.** But here's the trick: Make the time period short enough that you will have to actually work toward your goal, but make it long enough to be realistic (so you won't give up before you've even begun).
- **A good rule of thumb for short-term goals is to allow yourself between 30 and 90 days.** That way, you will see your goal as something you can realistically complete within the time allowed, yet there will be enough time pressure to get you moving, working toward making it happen.
- **Be sure to write the time frame down alongside the goal.** Now it's official: You've made a commitment to yourself, so keep that commitment!

Long-term goals: attracting who you want

Once you're on the way to becoming that new you, it's time to begin focusing on your second, more long-term goal. You will commit, in the next 6 to 12 months—however long you think is reasonable—to attracting people, you're interested in getting to know.

While this may seems like its own independent exercise, remember that this goal is closely related to your short-term goal of becoming more alluring. For one thing, you will have little luck attracting someone if you haven't honed your own attractiveness quotient. Conversely, you will want to enhance those qualities in yourself that will be desirable to the kind of people you are looking for.

For example, what if you are really hoping to meet and begin a relationship with a very basic, salt-of-the-earth-type person? You probably don't need to worry about learning the sociopolitical statements that are woven throughout Shakespeare's plays, but you will want to focus on more fundamental knowledge, like the best place in town to go for a steak.

The flip side of this is that if you focus your development on learning these more fundamental tidbits of knowledge, you aren't going to have much luck attracting a devoted academician.

A good fisherman learns what bait works best for each kind of fish he wishes to catch and uses the bait most likely to attract the fish being sought. Granted, attracting a romantic partner isn't as rudimentary as catching fish, and seductiveness should be much more than bait; but the basic principle is the same for both activities.

Here's how to create your long-term goals for attracting people:

1. Form a general picture in your mind of the kinds of people you want to attract. At this point, don't get too specific, such as listing each physical attribute you find attractive and eliminating everyone who lacks any of those attributes. (Such a practice will pretty well ensure that you will remain alone, and most people who engage in this practice do remain alone—not because they are too picky, but because they are afraid to get close to someone. The "pickiness" is, in the final analysis, just an excuse.)

2. Write a list of the characteristics you find attractive and by which you rate someone's seductiveness quotient. It's often difficult to do this at first, but once you start writing, you will probably find that you can't write fast enough to list the elements.

3. After you've made your list, set it down for a while. Get away from it long enough for it to "cool."

4. When the list has "cooled" enough, read it over, and ask yourself which elements on your list are really critical to you and which are less important or even inconsequential. Put a star beside the most important items. This is your "pass/fail" list.

5. Imagine a type of person who passes all your critical criteria. When you get a good picture of that type in your mind, expand your mental picture a little, and imagine what that person would be doing in his or her spare time.

6. Expand that mental picture a little more, and imagine where the person would be pursuing that favored activity. You now have a clearer picture in your mind of where to go to find these attractive folks. We'll go into that in a later chapter, but for now, know that you've taken the important first steps.

7. Finally, write down your goal. For example, "Within the next 90 days, I am going to meet six attractive new people. To accomplish this, I will do the following…." Follow with a short list of action items such as, "Beginning this Friday, I will start going to the weekly Singles Night at the local bookstore-coffee bar."

Once again, you've made a commitment to yourself. Keep it.

You can get there from here: putting your best self forward all the time

As you begin to develop your seductive new self, you are bound to face a few setbacks. I mentioned earlier in the chapter that the thought of reinventing yourself can be pretty daunting. It can seem even more so when you first begin to "try your wings" with your newly refined persona. Here are some guidelines to help you through the transition period:

- Don't get discouraged when you find the "old you" looking back at you from the mirror. That "you" is still a part of the new person you are creating, it's just improved.
- Remember that one of the biggest challenges to the newly emerging, the alluring person you are becoming will arise when you come face to face with someone who is intimately familiar with the way you were before. Just as we have the tendency, as adults, to revert to our roles as children when we visit relatives, we also tend to allow our old attitudes to emerge when we reunite with old friends and lovers who knew us "then." Before we know it, the new, improved "me" evaporates, leaving only the person we have been trying so hard to outgrow. The good news is that just being aware of this tendency will help you overcome it.

31

- If you have tried to change so much that the "old you" is completely hidden, you will naturally come across as being false, and your old friends will see it (and probably call you on it). Remember, if your true friends can see through your new persona, it isn't really for you, either. It is a mask you have put on to hide the "old you," and anyone you meet will eventually see through it, also.

Don't try to become someone else, just become the most desirable you that you can be.

CHAPTER 3

Physical Attraction: Looking seductive

The first element of seductiveness is your physical self. Whatever those enlightened folks may say about how unimportant physical appearance is, let's face it:

1. Your physical being is the first thing people notice when they meet you.
2. Your appearance is going to make an impression, one way or another.
3. You may think you don't have a lot of control over your fundamental appearance, short of paying a visit to a plastic surgeon.

In truth, however, there are plenty of things you can do to enhance the looks you were born with. Accentuating your good points while minimizing that characteristics you consider flaws is a common practice, not to mention the basis for a multibillion-dollar cosmetics industry. So let's begin building that altar of desire you're going to be.

Is your presence a sensual delight or a sensory assault?

To become as physically alluring as possible, begin with an honest appraisal of your looks. Be thorough but don't be overly critical.

The best way to start is to divide your physical presence into two distinct categories: what you like and what you're not so fond of.

Start by rating your face. This is the first part of you that most people will notice. (In a little while, we'll discuss body image and self-appraisal so concentrate on your face for now.)

- **Stand in front of a mirror and really look at your face.** Don't protest that this seems vain, you know very well that when nobody is around, you will gaze into the mirror, testing out new expressions and making sure that the old ones look the same as they did the last time you checked. At least now you've been given permission, and you're doing it for a real purpose. Look at your eyes, nose, mouth, and the texture of the skin. Pretend the image you see in the mirror belongs to somebody else and that you're evaluating the elements to determine how they look to you.

- **After you're done with the visual appraisal, make your list.** Divide it into two columns: "Enhance," which is the features you like, and "Refine," the features you think need improvement. Perhaps your favorite feature is your mouth. You see a deliciously sensuous, sexy, kissable mouth. (And, yes, men and women can both have sensuous mouths, so lighten up, guys.) Your mouth definitely qualifies as an enhanceable element, so write it down on that side.

- **On the "Refine" side, you might write down that you're not fond of your eyes because you wear glasses.** Maybe you heard the term "four-eyes" a little too often when you were a kid, or maybe someone you didn't particularly like wore glasses, and you can't quite kick the association. For whatever reasons, the glasses are a bummer for you. So on one side of the list, you've got those eyes that don't do much for you but on the other side, you have those gorgeous lips.

- **Decide what to do about the items on the "Refine" side of your list.** (The features you like, of course, you'll leave alone. If it works, don't fix it, right?) As was the case in your decision to become seductive, you'll probably find that goal setting will help you make the desired changes in your appearance. In some cases, only a short-term goal is necessary, and long-term goal setting won't necessarily apply.

There are some things you can do one time that will make a significant difference. Suppose, for instance, that you don't like your glasses. The short-term goal here is to get contacts. If you can't wear contacts, you can simply buy a better-looking style of glasses.

If, however, you want a long-term solution that involves neither contacts nor glasses, you might look into some of the newer and safer surgical techniques for correcting visual impairment. If you and your doctor decide this option is right for you, but you can't afford it now, this could be one of your long-term goals.

I want to share with you the stories of two of my friends. We'll call the woman Julia and the man Harold. Like most of us, Julia and Harold were not entirely happy with their appearances. But by being honest in their self-assessment and making a series of short- and long-term goals, they were able to recreate themselves and increase their seductiveness quotient considerably.

Julia: Facing the truth

Julia assessed her face and decided that her best feature was definitely her mouth. She had pouty, sensuous Sophia Loren lips. Unfortunately, she wore thick glasses and always felt self-conscious about them. So Julia decided she would break down and get contacts.

She had always been afraid contacts would be difficult to put in, but her desire to become the sexiest woman she could be was strong and getting stronger all the time. So she forced herself to overcome her trepidation over putting her fingers in her eyes and got fitted with soft contact lenses. So she decided to go for blue contacts—deep blue. Yum!

Julia didn't want to wear her contacts all the time, so she also invested in a pair of very attractive eyeglasses. This brings me to another point: Don't fret if you're one of those people who can't wear contacts. These days, you can choose from an endless array of flattering lens and frame styles.

While Julia was analyzing her face, she decided her make-up needed an update. So off she went to a well-known department store, where she met with a make-up consultant who diplomatically let her know that her look was slightly dated.

Julia had a complimentary make-up redo and was delighted with the results. Yet she just couldn't justify spending hundreds of dollars on the exclusive cosmetics for sale at the counter. She thanked the cosmetic consulltant, and her next stop was the drugstore, where she bought many of the same textures and colors of make-up. Thus she was able to re-create the look at a significantly lower cost.

Harold: Right Hair, Right Now.

Harold had a great face, with strong and even features, but his hair really wasn't that attractive. Actually, what was left of it was just fine, except he was losing it at a rapid rate. So lately, he had resorted to the tried-but-not-so-true, "comb-it-over-the-shiny-spot" technique, which was highly unsatisfactory.

So, Harold made a short-term goal to get a different haircut. He had his hair professionally styled in a way that didn't try to hide the fact that he was becoming bald. In short, he got a newer, snazzier look.

"Someday, I may consider hair transplants, or maybe I'll try that new anti-baldness pill that they've come out with," Harold says. "But for now, I think I've made the best choice, and I'm happy with it."

Grooming and Hygiene

It's nearly impossible to come of age in our odor-conscious culture without knowing the basics about brushing, flossing, daily bathing, and using a good antiperspirant. I won't insult you by implying that you're other than fastidious in this area.

As for grooming, you're probably savvy about the essentials here too. If, however, you're well-groomed but still are not completely satisfied with your look, consider seeking assistance from someone whose profession it is to make people look good—a hairdresser or stylist, for example.

These professionals deal with hundreds of different people, each of whom has a unique head shape, face, and hair texture. They can determine which hairstyle will work for you, and they can help devise the proper hair care routine for you.

Between your description of your lifestyle (including how much effort you want to expend on your hair) and the stylist's experience, you should be able to come up with a style that looks great all the time. A stylist might even save you from trying something that looks great on

Fitness and Health

Everybody has his or her own idea of what an ideal physical body looks like. Some people think anything short of Greek God/Goddess perfection is completely unattractive. Other people, however, like the look of a few extra pounds on their significant other. So what level of fitness is right for you? The answer is, quite simply, whatever your best is.

Being healthy and fit doesn't necessarily mean being a gym junkie. What it does mean is the following:

1. You are approximately the right weight for your height and body structure.
2. You can function at your preferred activity level without tiring too quickly or hurting yourself.
3. You feel comfortable with your body.

It is profoundly disturbing to hear about some lovely young woman who dies, as a result, of an extreme diet, all because her self-image was so distorted that she always felt that she was too fat. Yet, in our culture, we tend to encourage this very scenario by perpetuating the image of the ideal woman as being svelte, even waiflike.

In recent years, critics have lashed out at the "heroin-chic" look of runway models, who look to all the world like strung-out junkies. But, equally heartbreaking is the person, be it a man or a woman, who wrecks his body, destroys his internal organs, and develops cancer at a young age, all as a result of taking steroids to "improve" the body's definition.

It's far better to take an honest but kind look at your body as it is (more on that in a moment). Then work toward making it the best it was meant to be, rather than trying to change it drastically and force it into some completely unrealistic image.

The key to making your body the best it can be lies in— you guessed it— sound nutrition and some form of exercise.

It is beyond the scope of this book to delve into the particulars of your nutrition program or exercise routine. But if you want to know more about nutrition and how this can influence self-love, I recommend another book I wrote: "In a Relationship with Food".

Meanwhile, be good to your body, and the result will be that you'll feel good about yourself.

It's better than you think: adjusting your body image

Let's check in on Harold and Julia again. In their own ways, each of them decided their body images needed some work. Both vowed to themselves to improve the way their bodies looked, but they were savvy enough to know they had to improve in their own eyes first and then in the eyes of those around them.

Similarly, each of us has to arrive at an image of ourselves that we are pleased with. Like Harold and Julia, we can make a significant change in how we see our bodies by changing something simple and, to outward appearances, insignificant.

Apply the "Refine"/"Enhance" list and the goal-setting process to your body image, as you applied it earlier to your face.

Stand naked in front of a mirror. (You knew this was coming, didn't you?) Take a good honest look at your body, but remember that honesty doesn't mean ruthless.

As you did earlier, make a list with two columns: "Enhance" (what you like) and "Refine" (what you don't like).

Look at the list and decide what you can do—now and in the long run— to minimize the effect of each item on the "Refine" side of the list. At the same time, take each item on the "Enhance" side, and figure out a way to accentuate it.

Even Cindy Crawford doesn't look like Cindy Crawford...

Like so many women, Julia dreamt of looking like a supermodel— specifically, Cindy Crawford. Then one day, Julia was fortunate enough to see Cindy, who is admired for her candor on one of the model's many talk show appearances.

Cindy made a comment that provided a near-epiphany for Julia and which I think should be made into a bumper sticker or T-shirt and handed out to every female over the age of 10: *not even Cindy Crawford looks like Cindy Crawford.*

Even though she acknowledges she's a beautiful woman, she admitted that many of her photos are re-touched to remove a little blemish she might have that day or to otherwise smooth or enhance her image.

In another example, actress Morgan Fairchild published a beauty book. This gutsy woman, who presents such a startlingly beautiful public image, included unretouched photographs of herself without make-up. The difference between the Morgan we see and the Morgan who wakes up in the morning is astonishing.

Does this make her less beautiful? Hardly. But it does show us that her beauty is not the same as it's presented on the television screen or on magazine covers.

The whole point is that you need to have an accurate, realistic image of yourself and that you need to hold it up to real role models for comparison. If you continually strive to look like an image that's computer-enhanced or airbrushed, you will always feel short-changed.

Chiselled or voluptuous?

When Harold and Julia began working on their goals to improve their bodies, one of the first goals they both set for themselves was to become more physically fit. I recommend you do this too.

You don't need to strive for a perfect body—if such a body even exists. Just aim to be healthy in whatever represents good shape for you.

Julia began to review the exercise programs she had followed in the past. She'd never been a big fan of the gym scene, so she decided to try something different. Since Julia had always been attracted to Latin music, she signed up for some dance classes and started learning tango and salsa dancing.

Now, instead of being an exercise drudge, she finds she is having a great time in the classes. Not only has she gotten in noticeably better shape, but she also finds that moving with the exotic rhythms and perfecting the steps makes her feel incredibly sensuous.

Julia has discovered another bonus to her new enthusiasm for Latin dancing. Having always been a bit on the voluptuous side, she used to lament that she would never be as thin and willowy as the models she saw in Vogue.

Her attractive tango instructor, Raul, has helped change all that. Coming from a culture that appreciates curves in a woman, the flirtatious attention Raul pays her has given Julia a different perspective altogether and a new appreciation for her own natural beauty.

Harold had always been a jogger. He liked running, but he didn't really like having a runner's body. Though he was becoming more fit, his body kept getting thinner. He decided to cut down on his running program and chose to supplement it with weight training.

Harold started with an instructor to teach him how to handle the weights properly, and he began lifting a small amount of weight three days a week to improve his muscle definition. He soon found that the blood pumping into his biceps, along with their steady increase in size, made him feel very sexy.

It's not how you look. It's how you feel

In no time, Harold found he didn't even think about the fact that he was losing his hair, and Julia discovered that, when she thought about her eyes at all, she thought of them as an asset instead of a flaw. And although Julia's and Harold's respective self-improvement regimens were certainly making them look better, what was most important—and what made them keep coming back for more—was that they felt better.

When you adopt a physical-fitness program, the secret to success is to focus on how it makes you feel. Sure, it's wonderful to experience the pleasure of knowing your endeavor is helping you to look great, too, but if that's only reinforcement, you probably won't stick with it in the long run. As Harold and Julia discovered, it's far more rewarding to find an activity that makes your body feel as wonderful as it's beginning to look.

Do what makes you feel sexy and vibrant

Can you see how Harold and Julia's examples can apply to you? As the two of them did, you can devise a regimen that will help you achieve your optimum physical condition, but that will, at the same time, be a source of pleasure all its own.

There are countless activities from which to choose. If you need inspiration, the next time you're out and about, browse the free-publications pins in stores and restaurants. Check out some of the catalogs for community colleges or no-credit classes. Classes in everything from samba lessons to sky diving. Your town or city probably has something similar.

When you are engaged in some activity you thoroughly enjoy, which also makes you feel better physically, your self-image and your overall sense of well-being will improve dramatically. And believe me, that is seductive. It is truly a win-win situation.

Doing a double take

If you've followed the suggestions in this chapter, you have already evaluated your physical attributes. But because you are, after all, a work in progress and because your perceptions, as well as your appearance, will change as you continue on your journey, I recommend a periodic reevaluation.

Take out your original "Enhance/Refine" list, if you still have it, or make a new one. Understand I'm not suggesting that you turn this into an obsession, but periodically reevaluating yourself is a wonderful way to gauge your progress.

Harold and Julia knew this. After working out for about six weeks, they each decided to zero in on their bodies again and really take a look at their physical attributes.

Harold thought his growing biceps were definitely his best asset. Then he took a closer look at his face and decided it was his other best asset. Julia still thought her pouty, sensuous mouth was her best asset but now her long legs caught her attention too, and she was pleased. Her involvement with dancing had slimmed her thighs and toned her calves.

Just for the record, Harold never gave a second thought to his thinning hair. And Julia, having long since chucked the bottle-thick glasses, was seriously beginning to think her eyes were actually quite captivating. The "Enhance" side of each of their lists was growing, while the "Refine" side was dwindling.

You wear it well

The day came for Harold and Julia when they decided it was time to get to work on their wardrobes. They had gained confidence in their looks and felt they definitely deserved better "packaging." Both consulted experts to help them with their new looks.

For evaluating appearance and advising on changes, Harold and Julia had several types of experts to choose from:

1. Image consultants advise clients on hair color, hairstyle, make-up, clothing, and accessories and may advise on posture, general appearance, and demeanor. Some offer both personal and corporate image consulting services.
2. Make-up consultants advise clients on the type, color, and application of make-up.
3. Color consultants advise clients on the choice of colors for clothing that will complement their appearance.

Harold went to a quality department store and spent some time with a fashion consultant there, who guided him toward styles that would look good on him. With a little guidance, Harold got a feel for his correct style and managed to stay within his budget at the same time.

Julia decied to hire a personal wardrobe expert. This turned out to be a good investment for her. Unlike Harold, who put so little emphasis on clothes that he didn't have any, Julia had a closet filled with clothes. However, many of them were completely wrong for her desired image.

The first thing the wardrobe expert did was to clean out Julia's closets, leaving behind only a bare minimum of the best outfits. Anything that Julia hadn't worn in over a year or that she truly didn't feel good in was disposed of.

The consultant divided the remaining outfits into three categories:

- work clothes
- party clothes
- and play clothes

and told Julia to keep at least three or four outfits in each category that she felt extremely good in. She also took a very good look at Julia's coloring and told her that, while her closet was full of neutral colors, she was an animated person, and that brighter colors looked better on her.

What a difference this advice made.

Julia found that simply changing from brown to red changed the entire look and color of her complexion. Her overall appearance changed from that of a mousy wallflower who was easily overlooked to that of a striking, dynamic woman who made a statement.

Whether you choose to consult an expert or decide to go it on your own, here are some guidelines for buying clothes:

1. **Buy clothes that fit you well and are comfortable**. This is one cardinal rule that is every bit as important as style—perhaps even

more important. While tight pants may be sexy on a man or a woman, the effect is completely diminished if you have to keep tugging and pulling because they don't feel right, and a "wedgie" isn't sexy on anyone. Better that you buy your clothes a size or two larger so that you're comfortable in they and they hang properly without your constant attention.

2. **Select fabrics that feel comfortable.** I'm adamant about this point. A sensual person will have nothing touch the skin that doesn't feel delightful. It's better to wear a soft, cotton-blend sweater than a wooly one that really itches, no matter how good the woolly one looks. You have to feel good in the fabrics.

3. **Opt for quality over quantity.** Instead of trying to fill your closets, concentrate on buying clothes that fit well, are stylish but not faddish, and fill your senses with delight.

What the Sirens knew

Have you ever met someone who, at first appearance, was breathtakingly gorgeous, only to have that image completely destroyed the first time he or she spoke?

I bet most of us can name a few TV or film stars—male or female—who are extremely attractive physically, but when they speak, their voices are distinctly nonseductive. Of course, many "everyday people" have vocal challenges as well. Here are some common symptoms of an untrained voice:

- Some women take on a nagging, whiny, complaining tone. A man who hears such a voice will associate it with a woman who's impossible to, please. This is definitely not seductive.

- Some men assume a staccato tone—an impatient, aggressive manner of speaking that can come across as domineering, condescending, or arrogant.

- Some men and women have a tendency to just drone on and on. Their normal conversational tone is expressionless, flat, and dull. Either way, it's a turn-off.

- Some men and women may have problems with nervous or careless speech patterns: speaking too rapidly or too loudly, mumbling, and so on.

After our physical appearance, our voice is the most predominant feature we bring into our exchanges with other people, so it's important that we learn to sound as attractive as we look.

Both Julia and Harold decided to work on their voices. Julia hired a voice coach. Her coach helped modulate her voice, eliminating its slightly nasal quality. She also taught Julia various techniques to control her voice when she was nervous— techniques Julia was able to put to use right away when making presentations to clients on behalf of her ad agency.

Harold simply started to record his own voice and play it back, really listening to how he sounded. He also worked on eliminating his monotone speech pattern by trying to add vitality to his voice.

Before long, both Harold and Julia found their voices had become more resonant, more animated, and generally much more pleasant to listen to.

As a result, they also found that other people seemed more interested in what they had to say.

To evaluate your voice, here's a simple exercise to try. Do this whether or not you plan to hire a voice coach:

1. Record and listen to your own voice. Use a tape recorder, or simply listen closely to your voice message on your phone answering machine.
2. Ask yourself if this is the voice of someone to whom you would like to listen. Make a list of the qualities you think you need to improve. If you're not sure, ask someone else whom you feel can give you constructive criticism.
3. Record your voice again, and then again, until you sound "right" to yourself or the friend you've enlisted to help.

You do not need to be a supreme baritone or an exquisite soprano poised to take the opera world by storm. You simply need to enhance the quality of your speaking voice.

So, people will listen to what you have to say without being put off by the sound that carries your thoughts.

Knowing your style requires knowing yourself

The whole point of all this effort, and all these exercises, is to help you discover and polish your own personal style. You aren't trying to be something you're not, but rather to enhance and improve what you already are. Observe the characteristics you admire in other people, allow them to metamorphose to fit your own persona, and thus consciously develop your own personal style.

Perhaps your style is basic and earthy, perhaps it's glamorous, and perhaps it is constantly changing. Whatever your style is, it has to come from substance. It comes from knowing and being comfortable with yourself. Quite simply, you can't have a style of your own, and you can't do things that are truly unique to you until you have developed a level of confidence in and awareness of yourself.

CHAPTER 4

Intellectual Magnetism: Your brain is the most erogenous part of your body

It is well documented that the mind is the primary erogenous zone. Indeed, if you want to be seductive, your mind is the most powerful tool you have at your disposal.

There are two ways to put this tool to good use:

- You can program your mind with positive self-talk to convince yourself of your desirability—and once you're convinced, it's a breeze to persuade others.
- You can create a powerful mental presence that will make you irresistible. The key to creating this presence lies in sharpening your curiosity, seeking out new experiences, and deepening your zest for life.

What this chapter is really about is being seduced by life and embracing all it has to offer. A person who truly embraces life is unquestionably seductive.

What makes you sexy? Your thoughts

We've already talked about recognizing and accentuating your best physical qualities. Now, let's use that principal erogenous zone, your mind, and learn how to fully project those qualities. It's not enough just to be confident about that reflection you see in the mirror. Your entire attitude needs to be filled with the awareness of the glorious things you have to offer the world.

Let's look at some real-life examples.

Remember my friends Julia and Harold in Chapter 3? After Julia had been studying tango for a while, she found that she could easily imagine herself entering a room, awash in the sensuous beat of some Latin band. Every step she took, she was aware of herself as a lithe, hot-blooded dancer, poised to spring into movement.

And when she entered a room, you had better believe that she was noticed. Of course, she didn't actually burst into a tango, but the effect the image had on her attitude and, indeed, on her physical presence, was palpable. She had truly arrived.

Like Julia, our old friend Harold set his scene as well. But instead of being a slim, rather average-looking man who was losing his hair, he entered a room as someone who was physically powerful.

He envisioned himself as being somewhere between Arnold Schwarzenegger in Terminator II and Leonardo DiCaprio in Titanic, someone whose shoulder a woman could cry on, yet who could protect her from the villains of the world. And when he entered a room, you can bet his presence was felt.

You say you don't know the tango from the bus stop, your arms aren't pumped, and strutting just isn't your style? No problem! Find the qualities in yourself that you would like to project, and fill your being with them until you can no longer contain them.

All it takes is a little imagination and those exercises:

1. Pick a physical feature you especially like, perhaps from the "Enhance" side of one of those lists you made in Chapter 3.

2. Imagine that this feature brings incredible joy to the people around you and makes you positively entrancing.

3. Write an affirmation reflecting this thought. For example: "My gorgeous brown eyes cast a spell on everyone I meet, leaving them feeling that they must get to know me better." Don't worry if this looks a little corny on paper, it's for your eyes only.

4. Beginning now, whenever you meet anybody, think about your chosen feature in the glowing terms you've created. You don't necessarily need to repeat your affirmation fully condense it (for example, "Think eyes!").

This practice really works. Whenever you enter a room full of people, repeat two words to yourself: "Think lips!" As you begin to perceive yourself as more appealing, you begin to project that very appeal—and the people around you will respond to it.

Your intellectual presence

Now that you've established an alluring physical presence and have started to use the power of your mind to enhance it, the next step is to establish your intellectual presence.

Sure, you look great, and if you've been working on your voice (see Chapter 3), you probably sound better than ever—but that's not enough. To be truly seductive, you've got to have something interesting to say.

What is intellectual presence? It's a combination of several factors, including:

- **The way you think.** This is manifested in many ways, some of the most obvious being your opinions and your means of expressing those opinions.
- **The way you reason.** This is your ability to draw conclusions from the information at hand. Though this ability might vary depending on the situation, most of us are often at a middle ground between the cold and consummate logic of Star Trek's Mr. Spock and the artlessness of Forrest Gump.
- **How good you are at understanding other people's ideas.** Good listening skills are a must here, but beyond that, you should at least be capable of asking intelligent questions. A blank stare is not alluring.

These are all factors that make up your intellectual presence. But your powers of thinking, reasoning, and understanding simply do not develop in a vacuum. They have to be fed. Certainly, they are nurtured by your self-talk, but in order to give them a truly balanced "diet" you need to learn about things that are outside your personal arena.

Curiosity livened up the cat

If you want to be an interesting person, you first must be interested in many things. It does no good to be beautiful and have an entrancing, sexy voice if you have nothing of interest to say. What's one of your best tools to sharpen the old intellect? Curiosity, darling. Perpetually curious people are almost invariably fascinating and never lack interesting company.

A world of things to be curious about

There are some folks (not you, I hope) who constantly complain of boredom. To tell the truth, I've always been stunned to hear people say they're bored. In my opinion, boredom is an outgrowth of fear or simple laziness, or perhaps it is nothing more than a failure of imagination. Unless you are locked up in solitary confinement, boredom is almost never a result of there being "nothing to do."

To those who are chronically bored, I would ask you to consider this: There is a whole fabulous world just outside your door and an infinite number of absolutely fascinating things to do.

Your task, then, is to allow yourself to be seduced by the world around you, to be overwhelmed by the siren song of new ideas, experiences, and people. In the final analysis, nothing is more seductive than a person who has been seduced by life. And as for boredom…well, the cure for that can be summed up in three words: Look around you.

Get current

Simply broadening your perspective on current events makes a statement about your own level of interest and shows the person you're talking to that you are truly enamored of the world around you.

Although many of us get the fast-food version of the news from television networks, the "sound-bite" format of TV news reports just barely skims the surface of a story. For the most part, there's time for only the most sensational details of any given story.

To really understand what is going on in any arena, it's necessary to read, listen to, and see any and every source you can get your hands on. And yes, not only will you become truly seduced by life, but that seduction will be contagious, making you truly seductive to those around you ("Who is this interesting person?!").

Cultural seduction

Before we even begin discussing culture, I think it is important to clearly define the word. In this context, the typical image that comes to mind is one of the operas, classical music, Shakespeare, and those subtitled foreign films that many people pretend to understand but don't.

For many, even the thought of "culture" is off-putting. But the picture changes dramatically if you consider that culture is, by definition, any and all of the following:

1. A particular civilization at a particular stage
2. The tastes in art and manners that are favored by a social group
3. All the knowledge and values shared by a society
4. Refinement in tastes

"Okay, so culture is a lot more than snooty ladies with opera glasses," you may be saying, "but what does it have to do with seduction?" Well, as we discussed in Chapter 1, there are many ways to be seduced.

And some of the most profoundly seductive experiences take place not in bedrooms but in art galleries, museums, and even opera houses.

How about you? Even if you're not game for the opera, there are many ways to feed your hunger and broaden your cultural horizons. Treat yourself to these experiences:

- **Check out your local library or bookstore.** Walk into a library or bookstore and really look around. Think about how many books there are that you would like to read and how many you'll never read. Just for the fun of it, check out or buy a book by an author whose work you've never read but whom you've been curious about. Or try a completely different genre than you usually read. If you normally read nothing but science fiction, pick up a mystery or a book of literary essays. If you're a self-help-book aficionado, read a humor book for a change. But no matter which genre you choose, just for good measure, pick up a collection of literary erotica as well, such as Anais Nin's Delta of Venus.

- **Lend an ear to your favorite music store.** Go into a music store and look around at all the different kinds of music you've never heard. Sit in one of the listening booths and experiment with different categories of music to which you don't ordinarily listen. Suppose you're a classic-rock fan, try listening to some world music or something classical. If you're a jazz fanatic, check out some salsa or reggae. Then buy that "new" music, take it home, and listen to it. But don't just play the music, create a completely sensual experience for yourself. If you bought some hot Latin tracks, let loose with some sultry dance steps to match (and it doesn't matter if you don't know how to mambo, nobody's watching but your cat, right?). If you bought Yanni or Enya, light a few candles and some incense, step into a warm tub infused with aromatic oils and lose yourself in the ethereal world created by the music.

- **Meander through a museum**. Pay a visit to an art museum and really see the paintings and sculptures. Indulge your sensual imagination.

Guys, when you step in front of that Gauguin, don't just see a two-dimensional representation of a tropical scene; think of lovely and uninhibited Tahitian women slathering warm and fragrant oils all over your body.

Women, when you look at Rubens or Renoir, think of your own body being gazed upon by an artist and then lovingly recreated on canvas. (Oh, and don't forget to notice that the women in these paintings are not anorexic fashion- model types.) Beyond focusing on the purely sensual aspects of the artworks, make an effort to drink in the richness of the artists' experiences and feelings—and you will deepen the richness of your own persona.

Whenever you read a book, listen to music, or look at a work of art, try to feel the story behind it. Realize that behind every book is an author who has dreams, hopes, and hunger. Behind every musical score is a composer whose soul cried out for expression.

And behind each of these creators was a full life, perhaps lived in a time and place foreign to you. Simply by absorbing some of the seductive elements of the artists, and all the passions of their cultures, believe me, your own level of seductiveness will increase a thousandfold.

Outside the nine to five

1. Body painting?
2. Butterfly collecting?
3. Tarot card reading?
4. Tandem bike racing?

It doesn't really matter what it is—everyone should have a hobby. They're wonderful things because, by simply finding something that sparks your interest and passion—and then acting on that interest and passion—you are adding dimensions and facets to your personality that will enrich your life. Most likely, others will see and find your passion attractive, too.

Hobbies also give you confidence and increase your sense of self-worth.

How about you? What's your hobby? If you don't have one and don't have any overwhelming interest that you could turn into a hobby, think back to when you were a child. Recall some of the things you were interested in then.

Often, as adults, we put aside the things that excited us as children, yet our interest remains somewhere below the surface. Just acknowledging and rekindling that long-forgotten passion can awaken in you the endearing qualities that will make you more desirable to other people.

Soul searching in Seoul

Robert Louis Stevenson wrote, "I travel not to go anywhere, but to go. I travel for travel's sake. The great affair is to move." And a great affair it is, indeed. Travelling to new places, and experiencing new people and different cultures will inevitably broaden your own perspective, making you a far more interesting person to be around. Just the fact that you are interested enough to seek out these new experiences adds to your appeal.

To me, travel is synonymous with education, adventure, and some of the most enchanting experiences life has to offer. I have seen many of the world's most intriguing places. Yet there are so many wondrous spots I haven't seen yet and want to (Australia and India are tops on the list).

When I meet someone who has traveled to these or other fascinating places, I feel immediately attracted to that person. Why? If he has been someplace that I'm interested in, they have some new perspective that I want them to share with me. If we have traveled to the same places, there is a common experience that we share, which can create an immediate bond.

And the travel doesn't have to be some costly, extensive journey halfway around the world. You'd be surprised how many even little day trips around your home area can provide in the way of meeting and getting to know new people and how different a culture can be only a few miles down the road.

So check the tour guides, call a travel agent, or just fill the car with gas and take off. There's a wonderful, exciting world out there, and maybe a whole new you, just waiting to be discovered.

Being genius enough to admit to ignorance

Think back to the most interesting people you've ever met. Remember, in particular, one who seemed especially confident and comfortable with him or herself. Was this person spouting information and ideas or enthusiastically listening to what you had to say? Did this person seem to have all the answers, or did he or she seem excited to hear what you had to say?

The plain truth is that we appreciate someone who has enough smarts to say, "I don't know. Can you tell me?" This kind of person knows how to make the people around him or her feel important and, by so doing, makes him or herself more desirable to be around.

Remember, sometimes, the greatest conversationalists are the ones who know when to keep silent and listen.

Think of yourself as a very flattering mirror. Let people see, in your eyes, an attractive reflection of themselves, and they will find you more attractive.

Here are a few clues to follow when you're trying to inspire someone to be interested in you:

- **Nobody likes a know-it-all.** Few people are as annoying as those who feel compelled to dominate a conversation by showing how intelligent, wise, or learned they are. Such a person is stating that what they have to say is more important than what anyone else has to say. And you would go out of your way to avoid such a person, make a real effort never to be one.

- **Everybody wants to be a teacher sometimes**. It makes people feel good to know they have something valuable to offer. Having the opportunity to broaden someone else's awareness is a real boost to self-esteem.

- **Learning and self-respect are not mutually exclusive**. People who are insecure and doubt their self-worth will lie down and die before they admit, even to themselves, that they are ignorant about anything. People with a healthy self-image, however, are more concerned with learning something new than with appearing to know everything. Since self-confidence is a significant part of seductiveness (and an all-encompassing storehouse of knowledge is not), it makes more sense to admit that you don't know something than to pretend that you do. Besides, when it becomes apparent that you really don't know what you're talking about (and trust me, it will), any semblance of allure you might have established will fly out the window.

Look at the world as your oyster. It is waiting to share with you its many wonders. You have only have to go look for them. Treat every day as if it were the most important day—even the only day you have—and go out and learn as many things as you can possibly learn.

Many of the principles of becoming intellectually seductive are simple, but most people forget them. Therefore, if you use them, you will stand out from the crowd.

With your desire to become more alluring, along with your ever-increasing understanding of these principles, you'll be attracting new and fascinating people in no time. Other people will want to be around you and will be eager to be seduced by you.

Next, we'll dig a little deeper and talk about those elusive emotional buttons that you need to push to make yourself more seductive. I think you'll be surprised: it's not as complicated as you might expect.

CHAPTER 5

Emotional seductiveness: Creating those warm, fuzzy feelings

One of the most important parts of being seductive is the ability to make the person you're with feel warm, emotionally secure, and even joyful in your presence.

Even if you're drop-dead gorgeous, if the object of your desire doesn't feel good around you—and doesn't feel a kinship with you that transcends physical attraction—you'll never develop a relationship beyond a short-lived and disappointing fantasy.

While making yourself more alluring on an emotional level is more difficult than changing your hairstyle or wardrobe, it is ultimately essential in your quest to become the most seductive person you can be.

What's your compassion quotient?

If you're emotionally seductive, people feel comfortable showing, their feelings around you, and vice versa.

The key to emotional seductiveness is compassion, which does not mean pity. Rather, it means an ability to see into other people's hearts and to put yourself in their shoes.

But compassion involves more than lending a sympathetic ear when someone is down. Compassionate people have the capacity to find the sparkling thread of humor in everyday life—not laughing at people, but with them. They have a unique ability to infect others with their sense of joy.

Gauge your own compassion level by answering "yes" or "no" to the following questions:

1. When you ask someone, "How are you today?" do you really listen if the answer is something more than the automatic (and expected), "Fine, and you?"

2. When someone expresses frustration or talks about a problem they're having, do you listen with your full attention, not giving advice unless it's specifically requested?

3. When your neighbor regales you with an anecdote of his toddler's newest accomplishment, do you fully listen and really hear his story—refraining from interrupting with a "one-up" tale about your own child or the child of a sibling or friend?

4. Your best friend uncharacteristically calls you at four o'clock in the morning, devastated because she's just found out her husband is having an affair. Do you provide reassurance and make a commitment to get together with her later that day—without revealing irritation that your sleep was interrupted?

5. Do you take care to "be there" for a friend who's just lost a loved one, even if you feel a bit awkward because you don't know exactly what to say?

6. When someone tells you about his or her reaction to an experience, do you listen and genuinely try to empathize, even though you would have reacted quite differently in the same situation?

7. Are you easily able to find humor even in stressful situations— even if it means laughing at yourself?

8. When you meet someone new, do you avoid making rash negative judgments or critical conclusions? Do you try to focus on the traits of the person that you really like?

9. Can you have a spirited disagreement or conflict with a friend and emerge with the friendship intact (perhaps even enhanced)?

10. If you can truthfully answer "yes", to all of the above questions, you have a healthy compassion quotient. If you hedged a bit on some of them, don't beat yourself up. There's no time like now to work on increasing your "CQ."

Feelings...nothing more than feelings....

Before you can feel at ease showing your feelings or allowing someone else to share his or her own feelings with you, you must be comfortable having those feelings in the first place. The truth is that virtually everyone experiences feelings with which they aren't comfortable, and that runs contrary to their ideal image of themselves. For example:

- Men are taught from a young age that being a man means being able to withstand pain without being decimated by it—or even expressing it. Consequently, even after all that hoopla back in the 1970s about the sensitive Alan Alda type, it's still a common male belief that crying is unacceptable.

- Women are conditioned by our culture to be agreeable and to hide anger. For this reason, many women (yes, even in this post-feminist era) tend to shy away from expressing anger or even disagreeing with somebody's opinion.

- All of us, male and female, have our arbitrary lists of "shoulds" or "shouldn't" about feelings. These lists stem from a combination of factors, such as our upbringing, the social and political climate we live in, or even the people we're trying to impress.

You're on your way to becoming comfortable with your feelings when you realize that feelings in and of themselves are neither right nor wrong. (Of course, it's important that you express your feelings in ways that aren't hurtful to yourself or others.)

As you become more at ease with your emotions, you will create a climate in which other people are comfortable with their feelings when they're around you.

Learning to listen: using your ears and your heart

The single most critical element of emotional seductiveness is the ability to listen to others, not merely understanding their feelings on an intellectual level but empathizing and "being there" with them.

Emotionally seductive people are phenomenal listeners

Of course, this principle doesn't apply only to talking with the bereaved. Practice the art of compassionate listening with everybody every day. Learn to listen with your heart, not just your ears.

Fools rush in, but seductive people listen

Let's look more closely at the dynamics of seductive listening. When someone is sharing a personal story, seductive listeners are truly attentive and don't immediately jump in with their own story as if they were your opponent in a storytelling contest.

Unfortunately, the latter method describes the way too many people "listen." All too frequently, when people get together and converse, whether, in groups or one-on-one, the conversation is weighted with the participants' desire for one-upmanship.

A seductive listener refuses to play the one-upmanship game. Suppose, for example, that you have just related the trials of a recent move. Rather than jump in with an equally or more horrible story about moving, the seductive listener responds with empathy.

For instance, what would be an example of a good listener's response to the above quandary? "That must have been very stressful for you, to be starting a new job, and have to move everything you own from New York to Tampa, with only two weeks to get settled. You must be exhausted. I would think that facing a major move like that would be overwhelming. You've come through it with more steam left than I would have had."

Such a response tells you this person has really listened to and empathized with you and, just as importantly, that he or she admires you. This one-two punch is more than most people can absorb without feeling very kindly toward the person who said it.

Learning how to "resonate" with someone

Okay, I know, this business of "resonating" with another person sounds like more of that New Age hooey we hear all the time nowadays. Behind the trendy-sounding rhetoric, however, there's a sound and powerful principle.

Originally, resonance was a scientific term. In human terms, it simply means this: When you describe a feeling, experience, or idea, the person to whom you are describing it fully comprehends and, to a degree, shares that feeling, experience, or idea.

A truly seductive person is one with whom the person speaking actually feels that resonance, which leads to the sense that the person is "with them" in the experience. Such a person validates his or her partner's ideas or feelings and thus helps validate the person's worth. This is done not with the feigned agreement but rather via honest empathy and compassion.

The operative word in this concept is "honest." Since the perception of resonance takes place on a near-subliminal level, it cannot be faked. If you try to fake it, the other person will probably detect the insincerity—and that will effectively overshadow any other wonderful qualities you may have.

If you really think about it, you will realize that there's no need to fake it, anyway. All you have to do is really listen to the person and imagine yourself experiencing a circumstance similar to that which he or she is describing to you.

There's no trickery involved, no deceit. All that is required is your willingness to be present with another person.

Laughter is the best medicine (and the best aphrodisiac to boot)

Humor and a sense of fun are not only healthy and healing, but they are also some of the most powerful aphrodisiacs in the world. Having fun, sharing laughter, or even just being silly together can add fuel to the fire of a new relationship and can restore the passion in a relationship that has lost some of its sizzle.

It's no exaggeration to say that laughter and joy can be more enticing to the opposite sex than a hard body or legs "up to there." And even if you can't tell a joke to save your life, it's easy to make humor a part of your life. Here are a few tips:

1. Learn to make yourself see the humor in everyday situations, even those that you'd normally find aggravating. There's almost always a funny side. Laugh, and the world might not always laugh with you, but you'll feel better. And a person who's laughing, or at least smiling, is infinitely more seductive and attractive than someone who's throwing a temper tantrum or who's just a plain old stick in the mud.

2. Share your gift of laughter with others—not in a way that they feel they are being ridiculed or laughed at but in a manner that brings them into your personal circle of joy.

3. Never be afraid to laugh at yourself. People who take themselves too seriously are not seductive. On the other hand, people who have the ability to find joy and humor in their lives, and to infect others with that joy and humor, are nearly irresistible.

To make others like you, like them

This statement sounds so simple that it could be easily dismissed, but it describes the single most effective way to endear yourself to others: Like them. Think about how you react to people who really like you. It's difficult not to like them back, isn't it? Doesn't it make sense, then, to believe that another person would react similarly to being liked?

The key word in this idea is the word "really." You reacted positively to someone who genuinely liked you. On the other hand, you probably cringed when you perceived that someone was only pretending to like you or liked you because he or she thought a relationship with you could be beneficial in some way.

It is important to remember this distinction because it can mean the difference between attracting others and sending them running.

You might wonder how you can possibly make yourself like someone and not come across as being false. Well, you can't just make yourself like someone who doesn't have some characteristics that you find attractive, endearing, and intriguing in the first place. But sometimes, you have to look for these traits. The following exercise will show you how you can "learn" to like someone.

Try this exercise with the next five people you meet:

- Really look at the person with the intention of finding qualities you like. Don't focus on what you perceive as the person's flaws but concentrate on positive characteristics too.

- Practice thinking of the person in terms of the good qualities you've discovered.
- Let your "I-like-you" attitude shine through whenever you're talking to that person.
- There is something likable, even admirable, in virtually everybody you meet. You don't ever need to fake it and pretend you like someone. If you have to fake interest in a person, why are you trying to attract him or her in the first place?

Emotional seductiveness creates a win-win situation

The whole process of really listening to and empathizing, resonating, laughing, having fun with, and genuinely liking another person serves to validate his or her sense of self-worth.

The most powerful—and the only positive—form of seduction is the kind that leaves the person being seduced feeling somehow enriched by the experience. To enhance another person's good feelings about him or herself and about the experiences he or she shares with you is the ultimate goal in seduction.

Equally important is that the act of seduction is a positive, enriching experience for both parties. True seduction is one that leaves both the seducer and the person being seduced smiling when they remember the experience.

CHAPTER 6

Spirit or essence: All the elements of seductiveness… and more

In this chapter, we're going to discuss an intangible yet very powerful aspect of your persona: your SPIRIT.

Abstract though this quality may be, it is crucial to your seductiveness. For although it is difficult to quantify, the spirit is the aspect of you that truly makes you sexy.

So, just what is spirit? Some people think of spirit as being synonymous with "soul," but for our purposes here, we're going to define it simply as your essence: *The mystifying ingredient that is the sum total of all the other facets of your being.* Your spirit is a blend of many elements:

- How you look
- How you move
- How you speak
- How you think
- How you feel
- How you express your feelings
- The presence you bring into a room
- Your intent—the motivation behind the other elements

But it is more than these. It is also the confidence you feel and the passion that drives you.

Spirit, in short, is who you really are.

Though this elusive essence is comprised of all the other aspects of your being, it is also the core from which those aspects are drawn. Being as impalpable and abstract as it is, the spirit is also the most difficult element of your persona to work on.

It can be touched only through one of its manifestations—one of the more obvious parts of your being—yet it responds to the elevation of other elements by being elevated itself as a by-product of your efforts.

In other words, anything you do to upgrade one aspect of yourself will have a positive effect on your spirit.

What color is your aura?

According to some spiritual belief systems, the aura is an energy field around a person that shines with colours determined by their state of being—their emotional, physical, and spiritual condition. We won't go into whether or not this belief is valid, but the general concept is useful for visualizing what your spirit or essence projects to the people you meet.

That's what you're going to practice doing in the following exercise: Think of a color that describes your spirit, and then decide what that colour means to you. (And it doesn't matter what the psychologists say or what the "aura experts" say, this is your exercise.)

So, pick a color, any color. If you're drawing a blank, here's a brief list to jog your imagination. Are you:

Red: Does that mean you're passionate and sexy or angry?

: Do you have a cheerful, sunny nature, or are you "yellow" in the sense of fear?

Blue: Are you calm and steady or melancholy?

Green: Are you peaceful? Envious? Obsessed with money? Or concerned about the environment?

Purple: Do you have a regal nature? Or is purple a spiritual colour to you?

Pink: Are you gentle and loving (traits usually considered to be feminine but certainly present in men as well)? Or are you seeing the world through "rose-colored glasses"?

Gray: Do you feel formless or have a cloudy self-image? Or does gray spell dignity and strength to you?

Black: Does black signify depression or mourning to you? Does it whisper of elegance? Or does it mean you're secretive, mysterious?

White: Does this simply mean colourlessness, or does it signify purity to you? Or do you think of white light as healing or soothing?

Now try the following visualization exercise:

1. First, look over the list of colors above. Remember this is your exercise, so if the meanings of the colors listed don't ring true to you, make up your own meanings. If your color wasn't listed, add it to the list, and give it whichever meaning makes sense to you.

2. Find someplace quiet where you can sit down and concentrate. Turn on some soft meditative music if that will enhance your concentration.

3. Close your eyes and imagine there is a radiant emanating from your person. Its hue and intensity are shaped by your being and your mood. What colour is it, and what does that color mean to you?

After you've found your colour, think about what it means to you. If the meaning is negative, realize you can change either the color or its meaning to you.

For example, do you see yourself as a "red," and does red signify anger to you? Then why not concentrate on changing to a neutral brown or a harmonious green? Or why not focus on red as a color of passion?

Once you've found a meaningful, positive color, how can you use it? Simply think about your color at different times during the day—perhaps during your quiet time (or your meditation time, if you meditate)—and imagine yourself beaming that hue out into the world for everyone to see. It's really just another way of projecting your essence.

Spirit, essence, or whatever you want to call it: it's what makes you, you

We've discussed all the individual elements of your persona, describing how you can polish and improve them to make you more alluring and seductive. While each of these aspects is truly important, it's the sum of all of them—the whole package—that comes across to the people you meet.

Just as a chain is only as strong as its weakest link, that whole package that is you are only as seductive and desirable as the least desirable of the individual elements.

When your physical, intellectual, and emotional parts are all working well, your intent is clear, and your self-image is healthy. Such a balance feeds your essence—which, in turn, magnifies the attractiveness of your individual qualities.

It's like a perpetual-motion process focused on making you a better, more desirable being. The more you elevate the separate aspects of your being, the more your spirit is uplifted, and the more it enhances the individual parts of your persona, which then… well, you get the point.

A well-developed spirit is that special something that turns an apparently ordinary-looking woman into a ravishing beauty or a marginally attractive man into a desirable hunk.

Self-Confidence: where does it come from?

While your self-confidence is certainly influenced by events in the outside world, ultimately, it comes from within you. But what is self-confidence? It is the belief that you can achieve your goals, perform well in completing the tasks you face, and deal with challenges without being overwhelmed.

It is a freedom from fear arising from the knowledge that you are a competent, capable person.

Self-confidence is also the awareness that the world is not filled with enemies and negative people. Those who lack self-confidence harbour the fear that each person or situation they face is a challenge to their safety or well-being and that they, being less-than-capable, will probably be harmed or diminished by the encounter.

The saddest part is that, by holding such a belief, you can actually make it come true.

This may sound exaggerated, but if you approach all people as if they are your enemy, your defenses go up, and you don't let anyone get close enough to be your friend. If you perceive a situation as an attack, those same defenses go up, and you're so busy concentrating on protecting yourself that you completely miss anything positive the situation may offer.

You need to realize that self-confidence doesn't grow in a vacuum. While some people seem to be supremely sure of themselves from birth, you can bet there were factors that shaped them and made them self-confident.

Increasing your self-confidence can help you overcome many of your fears. You can become more confident by learning or accomplishing something new, participating in appropriate support groups, or, paradoxically, by getting involved in activities that help you focus on something outside yourself.

Consider:

- **Participating in a sport.** Take a martial arts class or become an exercise enthusiast. Physical activity can make you fitter, healthy, and vibrant, which can increase your confidence dramatically.

- **Taking an adult education class.** Whether purely for the pleasure of learning or for professional advancement, continuing your education can make you much more self-confident. Taking classes also affords you a wonderful opportunity to meet new friends with interests similar to your own.

- **Attending a Toastmasters or similar group in your area.** These groups exist for one reason: to help people overcome their fear of public speaking and help them polish their speaking skills. Even if you don't plan to do a great deal of public speaking, participating in a Toastmasters group can do wonders for your self-confidence.

- **Taking an acting course.** Whether or not you're interested in acting as a profession, an acting course can help rid you of your shyness and inhibitions, and, who knows, it just might bring out the "ham" in you.

- **Spending time in a supportive social setting.** There are many groups to choose from, such as religious community groups or, depending upon your situation, one of the multitudes of support groups available.

- **Getting involved in community organizations.** Consider a neighbourhood watch group, a park committee, or a local board. Feeling that you are a vital part of your community can increase your self-confidence.

- **Getting involved in a cause.** Whether you choose an organization that is local, national, or international in scope, working for a cause you're passionate about will help make you feel that you're truly a part of the larger world and that you're making a difference. That can be a real confidence builder.

As your skills increase, your self-confidence builds.

Essential elements: character and intent

As long as we're focusing on the intangible elements of spirit or essence, we have to look at what are perhaps two of its most elusive facets: character and intent.

Character is one of those qualities that whole libraries full of books have been written about, yet the definition remains incomplete. In its simplest form, good character means integrity. It means having a commitment to a set of values devoid of manipulation and being rich with respect for yourself and for other people and things.

Some people believe character is one of those "either you have it, or you don't" qualities, but, like any other facet of yourself, it can be developed and enhanced. In the case of character, however, it's, not so much a matter of specific exercises as commitment. It is a process stripped to its bare essentials, and it works like this:

1. You decide you want to act with integrity.
2. As you act on that decision, it begins to feel more and more natural until that integrity is a part of your core.
3. When you become so accustomed to acting with integrity that you aren't even conscious of it, you have developed good character.
4. The intent is the conscious manifestation of your character. It is the definition of your desires toward other people and situations. Those with character will consciously choose to act in a way that is beneficial to those around them and, indeed, to their world. Such actions are guided not by some desired response to the action (or fear of reprisal if one's actions are not beneficial) but rather by the desire to act well for its own sake.

There is a Jewish tradition known as the mitzvah, which, simply stated, is an obligatory good deed. The performance of mitzvahs is not contingent upon a system of punishments and rewards. Rather, the idea is to do good and act with integrity simply because that is the right thing to do.

I feel that no matter what our tradition or background is, this simple idea of acting with integrity for its own sake is something we would all do well to adopt.

Sometimes, we have to look closely at the intent before we act to make sure we are striving for the highest good for all involved in a situation. It's easy to convince ourselves that we are acting for one reason when our real motivations are completely different.

About all, we can directly and consciously do about our intent is to become aware of it. If our intent is less than noble, it's best to question our motives before we act at all. If our intent is benevolent, however, we—and those on the receiving end of our intentions—can be comforted by the knowledge that we are acting in good faith, without ulterior motives.

And that level of comfort that you instil in others is a very powerful part of your seductiveness.

Self-Worth: the reflection of your essence

There is frequently some confusion between the concepts of self-confidence and self-worth.

Quite simply, self-confidence is how you measure your own capabilities, self-worth is a measure of something much more intrinsic.

It is your perception of your value as a human being. The two can either reinforce each other or can be opposed.

The process of boosting your sense of self-worth is probably about 20% introspection and 80% action. So consider what it is you like and don't like about yourself, then go about the task of improving the things you don't like and reinforcing the things you like.

Ask yourself: "What have you done that you're most proud of, and why?" Quite often, the answer is something you did that brought joy to someone else. So the more good you do for others, the more you'll have to feel good about. (Remember what we were saying about character earlier in this chapter!)

Sit down and make a list of those actions. Every time you will read them will make you feel good and proud.

Then ask yourself, "What more can I do?" And make a list of those too. This list will give you hope and reasons to do good again.

Just for starters, here are some ideas:

- Volunteer to work with children in the burn or cancer ward in the pediatric unit of your local hospital.
- Help out with babies born to drug-addicted mothers.
- Give some of your free time to a soup kitchen (and not just at Christmas—these facilities often have a problem with too much volunteer help on holidays).
- Do some volunteer work for local AIDS organizations. Help out at a hospice, take meals to AIDS patients, or help them care for their pets.
- Help out at a shelter for women who are abuse victims.
- Volunteer for a local literacy program.
- Run errands for elderly, housebound people, or volunteer at a nursing home. You don't necessarily need to find an organization that specializes in this—you probably have a neighbour on your street or in your building who could use a helping hand.
- Become a Big Brother or Big Sister.

- Get involved with a mentor program at your local high school or university.

In truth, there are many concrete actions you can take to improve your sense of self-worth. Everybody has something of value to offer, whether it be skills, information, or just encouragement.

The simple act of smiling at someone who doesn't have much to smile about not only makes the object of your good intentions feel good but makes you feel pretty good, too. And who doesn't love to be around someone who feels good? It's contagious!

Ultimately, your spirit or essence is just as obvious as a brightly lit neon sign that you carry with you everywhere you go. Only you can determine what your sign says to the people you meet. Carry a sign of confidence, of comfort, of good intent—and you will be remarkably alluring to the people around you.

CHAPTER 7

Seductive powers

Now that we've laid the groundwork for seduction, it's time to go out and field-test your seductive powers. We'll begin by taking a close look at what men and women find seductive in the opposite sex.

Next, because you have to get out and find the person of your dreams before you can seduce him or her, we'll discuss the pros and cons of the various "hunting grounds." No matter where you go, you need to know how to attract your "quarry" once you're there.

Toward that end, we'll go into the how-to's of the initial approach, the nuances of body language and other romantic signals, and the perils and pleasures of flirting.

Sooner or later, someone is going to catch your eye, or vice versa—and you're going to actually go on a date with that person. You'll find a step-by-step "survival guide" to the date—and how to use it to your seductive advantage—as well as a basic evaluation system to help you decide if you should go out with this person again.

After all, even if you're not looking for your soul mate right now, you certainly don't want to seduce (or be seduced by) someone who's not right for you at all.

The ultimate seductress: a man's perspective

The debate about what constitutes seductiveness in a woman has raged for thousands of years. You would think that, after all this time, we would have reached some sort of consensus on the topic, but we have not for a number of reasons.

In this chapter, we will attempt to describe those attributes that men really desire and find appealing in a woman, as well as those that can instantaneously turn her from being a siren into a pariah in a man's eyes.

The bad news is that women can sometimes do some of the things that turn guys off without even realizing they're doing them. The good news for women is that these behaviors or traits are easily avoided with little awareness.

The even better news is, despite what women have been led to believe, the traits men are genuinely attracted to aren't impossible fantasies or unachievable goals, nor are they confined to a physical appearance that only a few women can achieve.

You can use this chapter to help you come up with your personal assessment of your seductiveness. That way, you can enhance the traits that make you more alluring while minimizing (or even doing away with) those that can turn men off.

His description of a sexy woman

One of the first questions a man asks about a woman he's never met is inevitable, "What does she look like?" The typical female response to having such a question asked about her is to bristle at the notion that so much of her perceived value is wrapped up in her physical appearance.

Women who don't think they're attractive don't feel comfortable being compared to other women they believe are prettier. And really beautiful women are tired of men who can't seem to look past their exterior.

When you add the fact that physical attractiveness is such a subjective value, differing from man to man, culture to culture, and even time period to time period, the very notion of defining physical beauty becomes somewhat ludicrous.

Our concern in this book, however, is not to perpetuate a long-running historical debate but to provide the modern woman with some real clues about how to make herself more alluring to men in general.

While individual men certainly have their own unique preferences, some feminine elements seem to carry an almost universal appeal. We will concentrate on these elements.

1. So what is this "universal" standard of beauty if such a thing exists?
2. What are the common elements that are attractive to all men?
3. And, most importantly, how many of those can the average woman, who is not a supermodel (more than 99 percent of the females in the world), manifest in herself?

Heady questions, all, and the answers may well surprise (and encourage) you.

The real deal

Face it, very few of us have perfect, supermodel bodies or faces. While there may seem to be an overwhelming amount of evidence that falling short of such mythical levels of beauty is a real handicap, you do not need feel shortchanged. The women staring back at you from the pages of Elle and Vogue may be images of impassioned promises, but you, a living, breathing object of natural beauty, are that promise fulfilled.

Accentuating that promise and that allure is simply a matter of bringing your more appealing features into focus and drawing attention to them while minimizing those features that you feel are less attractive. Here are some hints (also refer to Chapter 3 on the physical elements of seduction):

- **Pleasing parts**. Focus on the part of you that you really think is attractive ("lips, legs"). If you are particularly proud of your legs, for example, you may want to wear dresses that draw attention to them. That doesn't mean you have to wear skirts so short that you can't sit down comfortably. Men actually prefer a skirt that is a bit above the knee, perhaps with a slit in the back. The quick glimpse of a little more thigh (and perhaps the hope of seeing a bit more) is frequently more tantalizing to a man than seeing everything all at once. Remember, men are visually oriented creatures, capable of intense fantasies. Inspiring those fantasies, even with a minimum of visual stimuli, can go a long way toward seducing a man.

- **Appealing apparel**. In all you wear, look for a proper fit and feel so that the garment makes you feel as good as it makes you look. Your clothes must allow you to move naturally and comfortably, adding to your sense of confidence as you wear them. In addition, your clothes need to look "touchable" to a man. While a crisply pressed business suit may communicate competence and confidence, your overall look needs to be less harsh than the common dictates of business attire. Run your fingertips across the fabric of your favorite outfits and ask yourself what the material is saying. Look at the cut of your clothes, and ask yourself what your overall impression is. Then ask yourself if these are the things you want to communicate to the men in your life. If the answer is no, it might be time to do some careful shopping.

- **Finishing touches—for maximum touchability.** The same approach applies to your hair and make-up. You want everything about you to look touchable, even inviting to a man's caress. Men have often told me that if a woman looks like the slightest touch would destroy her image, they simply won't want to touch her. In short, lose the shellac hairspray, ditch the three coats of industrial-strength mascara, and strip off few layers of rouge. In addition, if you tend to trowel on the foundation, give the trowel to your favorite bricklayer. A man would much rather see a few real flaws than a perfectly applied coat of putty and paint.

"Drop-Dead Gorgeous" Defined

While men are, as a rule, visually oriented and are frequently quite verbal in describing what they find attractive in a woman, a little bit of probing reveals they are not as universally obsessed with specific parts of the female anatomy as one might think. When men describe their image of a beautiful woman, they may well begin by describing a full, well-proportioned bust line or a taut, toned bottom.

Almost, without exception, however, they go on to describe the woman's eyes and how those eyes seemed to beckon with some hidden promise. Other times, they go into great detail, describing a smile that held laughter even in its silence or soft, pouting lips that seemed to beg to be kissed.

When you ask the men for specific details, such as the color of the woman's eyes or the actual physical shape of her mouth, they seem to falter a bit. It seems that they are enthralled not so much by the actual physical characteristics as by their own interpretation of what those characteristics represent.

In short, they are describing the spirit behind the physical.

You may be thinking, "Great! I can work on the shape of my butt and wear clothes that enhance my bust line, but how in the world can I change what the shape of my lips 'says' to a certain man or what the color of my eyes communicates to him?"

Here's where the really good news comes in. While you can (and should) continue to work to keep your physical body in healthy condition, you can have an even more significant effect by working on your attitude.

Tell yourself what a mouth-watering morsel you are, and imagine every head in the room turning to admire you as you enter. Like Julia in Chapter 3, you can imagine your every move to be a sensuous dance. Imagine your mouth uttering some profoundly seductive promise to the ear of every man in the room. Imagine your eyes saying, "Perhaps..." to every gaze you meet.

And when you're actually with a man, focus all those promises of untold pleasures upon him alone, as if he were the only man in creation. Again, by seducing yourself, you are seducing any man who comes in contact with you, even from across a crowded room.

Here is an exercise you can use to hone your self-image and prepare yourself for your "grand entrance:"

1. Take a long, leisurely bubble bath, adding your favourite fragrance to the bath water. You might even want to light some candles and turn the light off. Put some sensuous music on the stereo, perhaps Sadé, Leonard Cohen, or some jazzy Billie Holiday. As you sink into the warm water, focus on the sensations it offers your skin. Feel how it literally draws the tension from your body, and allow yourself to sigh softly as you give yourself up to the experience. As you wash your body, luxuriate in your own touch, focusing on each sensation as your fingers glide across your skin.

2. When you are finished, emerge from the bath with a brand new, extra plush bath towel. Pat yourself dry as you would have a lover do it, relishing in the softness of the towel upon your skin, as well as the suppleness of your body beneath your fingertips. Imagine how glorious that body must feel to a man.

3. After you are dry, splash on some refreshing cologne, making sure to apply it to all those places where you would want your man's attention to be drawn.

4. Standing before the mirror, illuminated by candlelight, gaze appreciatively at each part of your body, imagining your man's pleasure if he could see through your eyes right now.

5. Now, as you dress, let each article of clothing you put on be a conscious attempt to amplify your seductiveness. The garments

touching your skin must be soft and smooth as a lover's lips and must be as beautiful as the woman you wish to be. The outfit you wear must serve as a subtle but clear reminder of the seductress upon which they are draped. They hint at pleasures just beyond his reach, on the fringes of his dreams.

6. Apply your make-up carefully and conservatively. Imagine that your lips are the portrait of unspoken promise, adorned with the care of a Botticelli. Your eyes are their own deep pools of passion and need only a subtle touch to draw his attention to them. Once there, he will be lost in their allure.

7. After you finish dressing and venture out into the presence of the object of your desire, remember the sight of your own nakedness as you stand before the mirror. Hold the image of that sexy, seductive, confident woman in your mind, remembering that this beauty was no air-brushed super model—it was you, in all your glory.

Seductive is as seductive does

If you pay attention to the media nowadays, you probably assume that men think the most seductive women are 18 to 25 years old, wear as little clothing as possible, and have the inclination genetically implanted in their brains to hop into bed at the earliest possible opportunity. Such an assumption is not only frustrating and demeaning to most women, it is patently untrue.

So how does a woman have to behave to be considered alluring to men?

Does her every action need to scream "yes" to everyone she's with? Hardly. Remember that a man, like a woman, wants to feel valued and special. A woman who seems to be available to everybody she encounters may well be the object of his prurient fantasy but not of his prolonged attention.

A far more appropriate projection would be, "Perhaps...but only with you." To be truly seductive, such a statement would come from deep within her rather than being tattooed across her forehead.

Focus, Focus, Focus!

The first element in female behavior that men consider alluring is the woman's ability (and desire) to focus her attention on him and him alone. I'm certain every woman knows what it's like to be talking with a man who seems to be paying as much attention to other women as he is to her: It doesn't feel very good.

So why would we think that men like receiving the same treatment from us? Is it because they don't have the same feelings that we do? Of course not.

A Confidante...or the Town Tattler?

Another element important to a man is his need to be able to trust the woman he's with. He needs to know that she is being honest with him and that the stories she tells her friends about him will be consistent with what she says to his face.

He needs to know that what he says to her in confidence will remain their shared secret. He wants to be sure that if he shows her his more vulnerable side, it won't become an item for discussion around the coffee pot at the office.

This sounds simple enough, yet we women often damage that trust just by sharing someone else's confidence with him. We may think that we're letting him "inside" when we tell him about so-and-so's problems, but we're actually letting him know we can't keep a secret.

So don't say anything that could be construed as gossip, or he will close up like a bear trap and may never let you in again. Learn to be gentle and discreet in your descriptions of others, as gentle as you would want your man to be with you.

The spirit of the enchantress...making it or breaking it without lifting a finger

In the exercise earlier in this chapter, we demonstrated how a woman's attitude and her internal dialog could dramatically affect her outward seductiveness simply by making her feel more seductive. At an even deeper level, our attitudes affect the way we perceive the men in our lives and, thus, how we act toward them.

The key word in this whole process is intent. How we feel toward men in general, and the man we are with in particular, has a significant effect upon our behaviour, even in ways of which we are unaware. These attitudes may be the product of our past relationships or may even be deeply ingrained into the very fabric of who we were at birth.

Your intent toward another person is comprised of all your hopes, fears, past joys, and past pains. Though intent makes up a significant portion of a person's attractiveness and allure, people frequently give little consideration to what that intent is.

We want without understanding what we want. We seek tokens for reasons we never consider. It follows, sadly, that if we are unable or unwilling to consider our own real needs, it becomes natural for us to not consider the needs of our partners. Our intent toward the other person becomes narcissistic and destructive.

For better or for worse, your intent will be projected to the men you want to attract, either adding to or subtracting from your seductiveness quotient. Without lifting a finger, you can make or break the enchantment. The good news is that if you're projecting a less than enchanting persona, you have the power to change it. It's all up to you.

In the final analysis, we women are real winners in the seduction game because the better a man is at pleasing us, the happier he is. Just by enjoying ourselves when we're with a man, we go a long way toward ensuring that he is enjoying himself, as well.

And by feeling more seductive, more alluring, we actually become more alluring. No matter where you go, you aren't likely to find a better deal than that.

So go out, have a wonderful time, and dazzle the men in your life in the process!

CHAPTER 8

Romantic signals: How to read them and how to give them

Without even opening your mouth, you speak volumes of information to the people around you. The way you stand and si, your facial expressions and even the way you position your arms and legs serves to communicate your mood or attitude. And, of course, the people all around you are busily conveying their own nonverbal messages to you and anyone else who's paying attention.

Although most of us normally use such nonverbal forms of communication quite unconsciously, we can learn to modify the silent signals we send out. This is useful whether you're attempting to seduce that gorgeous man or woman you just met or you're trying to close a business deal.

I'm not suggesting you try to "lie" with your body language, just that you learn to observe what you're communicating. So that way, you can address—and, if necessary, modify—your attitudes. Similarly, you can learn to read the nonverbal messages of others around you.

This chapter will help you become more observant of body language in other people and in yourself. It will also help you ensure that what your body is saying is consistent with what you really feel. Realize, of course, that this is general information, and some of the nuances we discuss may vary from person to person and culture to culture.

Developing your "Body Literacy"

I can understand how intimidating the study of body language can seem when you first consider it. There have been quite a few scholarly—and a few less-than-scholarly—works that describe in detail what every posture signifies and what every gesture means.

While I have no desire to discount the value of all the work that's been done on the subject, I will say that you already know the most important information, even if you aren't consciously aware of it. It's very easy to "hear" what another person's body language is saying to you once you make a conscious effort to notice it.

Imagine, for example, that you are talking to someone, and you notice that she's keeping her arms folded tightly across her chest. Think about how you feel when you assume that same posture.

One reason you might do it is that you are cold, folding your arms is an attempt to keep in your body heat and keep the chills at bay. But you also might assume this position if someone is making you uncomfortable, perhaps by being overbearing.

Logically, then, if someone adopts this stance while talking to you, he or she is unconsciously trying to remain insulated from a source of discomfort. When you're confronted with such a situation, ask yourself what you might be doing or saying to make the person uncomfortable.

Another possibility is that the person is shy or self-conscious, and he or she stands like that as a matter of habit. (Then again, maybe it's just chilly in the room!)

When you're talking to somebody who's standing or sitting across from you, learn to really notice the person's position. Without studying the position of each hand, foot, arm, or leg, you can determine very easily whether an individual's overall attitude is one of openness or whether he or she is "circling the wagons."

Is the person leaning toward you as you talk or away from you? Are this individual's hands open, as if he or she were accepting a gift, or clasped, as if clutching a purse, protecting it from thieves? These descriptions may be exaggerations, but you get the point. There's no rocket science involved in interpreting body language, just common sense.

Eye contact: Magic or Menace?

We, humans, have long held that a person's eyes are the "windows to the soul" and we tend to place the great substance in how a person maintains— or avoids—eye contact during conversation.

It is here that the "reading" can get a little tricky. Some people simply aren't inclined to make heavy eye contact and tend to look away frequently. This doesn't necessarily support conventional wisdom, which says that such people are usually deceitful. The person may simply be shy.

By the same token, just because someone looks unceasingly into your eyes when he or she speaks doesn't mean this person is necessarily a paragon of integrity. On the contrary, deceivers may actually be consciously forcing themselves to maintain eye contact to convince you that they are truthful and/or interested. Or they may even be trying in some way to manipulate you or intimidate you with their steady, unwavering gaze.

Look closely into the eyes that stare into yours, and try to read what is behind them.

Other factors that can influence your interpretation may be the result of the individual's genetics rather than his intent. For example, it's said that someone with close-set eyes is somewhat shifty, or someone has "beady little eyes" if her eyes are small. While I am certain that each of us can recall someone who fits these descriptions (physically and in personality), to be fair, we need to at least consider our prejudices when we make our interpretation.

By using common sense and your instincts, you can get a pretty accurate idea about the person, regardless of how long he or she looks into your eyes.

Remember the foremost factor in seductiveness is intent, and the best way to read that intent is on an intuitive level.

Body talk: saying it without words

If it's important to know how to read body language, it's equally as important to know how to "speak" with your own body.

You probably know what you want to say. Now we're going to look at a few ways to say it clearly, without uttering a word.

Keep in mind that this isn't about deception, and it's not about engaging in the sort of forced posturing that's as obvious as a rhino in a phone booth.

Instead, what we are trying to do is make you aware of what your body language is saying, so you can be certain that it mirrors what you really feel.

Just, as you choose your words when you are describing a situation to another person, you can also choose your body language. This isn't being deceptive. It is simply exercising your communication skills to describe your thoughts as accurately (or sometimes as diplomatically) as possible.

Leaning with meaning

Have you ever been talking to someone and noticed the individual leaning forward in his or her chair as if ready to pounce? Did you feel as if the person was really excited about what you had to say?

Though you don't want your partner to feel like wounded prey faced with a hungry predator, you do want to physically convey your interest. Leaning toward someone says, quite simply, that you want to be closer while leaning away lets that person know that you'd rather be somewhere else.

Positions the Kama Sutra never mentions

The way you position your body, especially your arms, hands, legs, and feet, can give someone a fairly clear indication of how you feel in his or her presence. At the same time, you can't (and shouldn't) try to lie with your body—any more than you should lie with your words—you can choose to be conscious of how accurately your position communicates your feelings.

Think about whether you do any of these things:

- Do you assume a position that looks defensive, even though you're sitting with a person you like? Is this because you're shy or self-conscious, or because you have something on your mind that is adding to the stress of meeting someone new?
- Notice your hands. Are they open, as if waiting to accept a gift, or clenched tight, as if you were holding your last dollar in a room full of pickpockets?
- If you're a woman, are your legs so rigidly slammed together that they're screaming, "You're never getting in here!" or are they more relaxed, saying, "I have no need to protect myself from you."
- If you're a man, are you hovering over the woman you're interested in as though you're about to pounce on her—and is she subtly but progressively drawing back and looking around as if she's plotting her escape?

While I have presented some extreme examples here, you should ask yourself where your body talk falls on this spectrum.

Smile without guile

1. **Smiling is one of the most dynamic forms of body talk**. When you smile at someone sincerely, you're telling the person that you are enjoying the time you are spending together.
2. **When a woman smiles**.... It is especially true for women that a smile goes a long way toward seducing a man. He wants to please you and may even have a lot of his own self-image tied up in his ability to please. Therefore, when you smile at him, you're telling

99

him that you're enjoying his company and that he's doing all right with you.

3. **When a man smiles**…. A man's smile can communicate the same acceptance as a woman's, but his intent has a bigger effect on how the smile is interpreted. No woman likes to feel as if she's an horse d'oeuvre on a plate, waiting to be consumed. She wants to feel wanted, even lusted after, but she wants to be desired as a whole person, not just as a repository for a man's lust. So ask yourself, guys, whether your smile is expressing your appreciation for the person in front of you or for the person you hope will be writhing around naked later on. It really makes a big difference.

Eye gotta be me

Since we've already determined that the eyes are the windows to the soul, it makes sense to be conscious of what your eyes are saying to the other person. The phrases "bedroom eyes" and "undressing her with his eyes" are good descriptions of some of the things your eyes can communicate to your partner.

They speak so clearly of your intent—and your spirit—that they can deafen your partner to what you might actually be saying.

If you look at the person you're with and find yourself thinking that he or she is absolutely delightful, that delight will shine like a neon sign in your eyes. If you're looking at the person, however, and thinking this individual is the answer to all your emotional needs, that person will inevitably see you as some kind of emotional vampire, waiting for the opportunity to drain all of his or her energy.

Beyond the intent behind your eyes, how you physically focus on someone has an effect on how you are perceived. You want to look into the other person's eyes while you are with him, but not with an unbroken stare.

Look away from time to time, and allow the person some emotional space. You might even look at the person's hands sometimes while she's talking to you, as the hands provide animation to the dialogue.

Animated Annie or Wooden Wanda?

Consider also whether your responses to your partner's conversation are animated and alive or stagnant and dead. If you look as if you're bored with someone, that person will give up on you in a hurry.

An advice: Don't get all carried away with this animated-response principle, or you'll look like a puppy greeting its master at the door after a day-long separation. That can be scary to anybody. Find a middle ground—one that expresses your interest but doesn't make you look like a blithering nincompoop.

Act toward that person as you would toward anybody you find interesting. Keep your eyes on him or her during the conversation, smile often, and nod when appropriate—in short, make it apparent that you are really listening to what this person is saying and that you genuinely enjoy being in his or her presence.

The proper use of props

Yet another way that you can seductively communicate without saying a word is through the use of props. Now, I know this sounds really staged, but it's something we all do unconsciously. I'm suggesting you to make yourself conscious of your movements and use them to your advantage.

Men, imagine you're sitting across from a very lovely woman, and both of you seem to be enjoying each other's company. You notice that her fingers are moving ever so delicately, up and down the stem of her wine glass.

What comes immediately to mind?

With this subtle movement, she has increased the level of your interest, and you find yourself fantasizing about her. (Women, are you paying attention to this?)

I have also heard that some women have an equivalent response to a man who lightly (and apparently absent-mindedly) runs his fingertip around the rim of his glass, occasionally even touching his finger to his lips to moisten it. There is any number of ways that you can inspire your partner to fantasize about you without being crude or even obvious. Use your imagination.

Once you do, you'll find any number of props you can use to seductive ends. Again, subtlety is the key. Use what's on hand, don't go out of your way to find a suggestive object. After all, you want your actions to be smooth and natural.

The wine glass suggestion I mentioned earlier is a good example of a sensual prop, and there are many other objects you can use: a pen, a straw, a scarf, or lipstick, for example. A woman playing with her hair can convey a seductive message to the man sitting across from her. A man gently running his fingers over his silk tie can send a sensual message to his partner.

Be playful, and, by all means, have fun with props. Don't fiddle with them nervously, however—that's not sensual.

Seduction: it's more than mental—it's also a contact sport

Despite what some people may think, foreplay begins long before any clothes start coming off and even before any decisions are made about having sex. At that time of Exquisite tension when neither person knows where a relationship might go, even the slightest contact can be a source of sparks or revulsion.

Intent and finesse are what separate the two.

Since the brain is the primary erogenous zone, your initial acts of seduction must be more mental than physical. The whole idea is to get your partner thinking about you in a sexual light and to enjoy those thoughts. As I've said so many times before, your intent will be communicated very clearly to your partner.

If all you're interested in is a sexual encounter, all your words and deeds will carry at least a subtle undertone that your partner will hear and see. If, however, you see your new partner as an emotional, intellectual, and even spiritual delight, as well as a potential romantic and sexual partner, that balance of intent, will also come across.

So how do we turn up the heat without getting burned?

Certainly, a spontaneous grope for your partner's more personal parts would be counterproductive. It is here that your finesse plays such a crucial role.

→ You want your partner's passion for building slowly to a fever pitch.

→ You want this person to be excited about exploring new experiences with you.

→ But you want this person to feel as if the seduction is his or her idea.

So you plant little seeds. If the situation is right—and the chemistry is there—these seeds will blossom.

Some of the most effective seeds you can plant take the form of sensuous touches. They seem to be completely spontaneous, done almost absent-mindedly. Yet they are very effective in sparking thoughts in your partner's mind.

It is impossible to overstress the importance of intent and finesse where the art of sensuous touching is concerned. Perhaps more than any other aspect of seduction, there is a very fine line between what is welcome and alluring and what is unwelcome and even offensive.

You need to be very conscious of your partner's boundaries and respectful of his or her concept of personal space.

Some people think nothing of giving a peck on the cheek, embracing, or being embraced by a new acquaintance, while others reserve any physical contact whatsoever for people with whom they already feel intimate.

Go slowly with your attempts at physical contact and read your partner's reactions every step of the way. If you do it right, your sensuous touching can lead you both into a truly delicious seduction.

You have at your disposal many different tools that you can use to communicate with your partner. You may impress someone with your words, dazzle him with your smile, and mesmerize her with your eyes. With the right little touches, you will complete your delicious seduction.

Always remember, however, that a seduction that doesn't make both of you feel good is not worth pursuing.

CHAPTER 9

Flirting: Tickle, tease, or torture

At one time or another, nearly everybody has flirted with someone they find attractive. For many people, flirting is nothing more than a fun and harmless way of interacting. But flirting isn't always harmless, and it can sometimes be quite destructive.

On the other hand, it can also be a powerful prologue to that delicious seduction we all long for. It depends on upon several factors:

- your intent,
- the other person's expectations,
- and the actual results.

In this chapter, we'll explore the different types of flirtation, and I'll share some pointers on how to flirt seductively.

The flavours of flirting

Webster's dictionary defines flirting as "acting amorously or seductively without serious intent." But just as the word "seduction" has changed in meaning over the years, "flirting" has undergone a similar transformation. It no longer necessarily means acting without serious intent, although it certainly can mean that. Let's begin by defining our terms.

There are three kinds of flirting:

1. **Harmless flirting**. I like to think of this as equipment-check flirting. It's just a way of testing one's attractiveness to the

opposite sex, with no serious intent, but with no harmful results either.

2. **Destructive flirting.** Maybe it's a woman who comes on to every married man at the party during the wives stand around seething. Perhaps it's a married man who flirts constantly and outrageously with other women, even (or especially) in the presence of his wife. Or maybe it's your blind date, who's too obviously not blind whenever another attractive woman walks by your table. If flirtatious behavior causes discomfort, anger, or unhappiness, it is destructive. The destructive flirt may not necessarily be flirting with harmful intent, but he or she is flirting without regard for the results.

3. **Seductive flirting.** This is meaningful flirting. It's flirting with a serious purpose, and that purpose is pleasure (without pain).

Before we discuss the different types of flirting, I want to say few words to those of you who have cold feet about the whole thing. I know you're out there, so come on in, sit by the fire and let's get you warmed up.

Hope for the Flirt-O-Phobe

Many people have anxieties about flirting, and as a result, they don't do it well, or they don't do it at all. If so, they may be missing out on a lot of fun. For, despite my many caveats about destructive flirting, the truth is that harmless flirting can be fun, and seductive flirting can greatly enrich your seduction experience.

Most people with flirting anxiety are simply afraid of rejection.

The good news is that much of this fear can be overcome by shifting your mind from the idea of flirting to the idea of simply connecting with another person.

When you connect with someone, you make a link or a bond with that person, and not necessarily with romantic or seductive intent. You can make a connection with the gas station attendant, the person in line behind you at the supermarket, or the woman who's checking you out at the bookstore (by this, I mean she's ringing up your purchase, not "checking you out" in that way).

In fact, connecting with people in these neutral situations is a great way to begin getting over your anxiety about flirting. After all, what is flirting but just another way of connecting with other people?

I'm going to share some secrets for connecting. Master these, and flirting will come naturally.

- **Your state of mind is the most important determinant of your happiness**. Your happiness doesn't depend on your state of matrimony or relationship, it depends on your state of mind. Seducing someone that you're wild about may ultimately be your goal, but remember, getting there is half the fun. And you do want to have fun, don't you? Otherwise, what's the point? Whether you want to be a great seductress or seducer, or you just want to form a connection with that woman who works at the bookstore, cultivate a joyful state of mind, and the rest really will come easily.

- **Don't be too attached to the outcome of your connection attempts.** When you're connecting with someone or even flirting with that person, you're not going to hit the mark every time. It's like striking a rock 99 times, and it doesn't crack until the 100th swing of the pick axe. You need a little practice, particularly if you haven't been out there flirting in a long time (or ever). Remember, you're going to start simply by connecting, making conversation, and talking to people. Learn not to be disappointed if the outcome isn't exactly the way you would have liked.

- **Remember that everyone wants to connect with a happy, confident person.** Do whatever it takes to reinforce your confidence and your self-esteem. Remind yourself that you're a unique and worthwhile person. If you need some inspiration, go back to some of the exercises.

- **Smile!** It sounds so simple, but if you learn the art of a genuine smile and practice it as often as you can, people will be drawn to you. Try smiling at people whom others rarely smile at—that grouchy librarian nobody, ever talks to, the post office attendant stuck behind the service counter at lunch hour, or that check-out clerk in your supermarket who looks like she's never smiled a day in her life. See if you can't light up that person's eyes. When you smile, you give away a gift of joy.

- **Practice eye contact.** But practice it in moderation, you want to look interested, not predatory. Look away occasionally when you're talking to someone, but do return your glance frequently, and be sure to smile.

- **Genuinely care and have empathy for the people with who you're connecting.** If you make a genuine attempt to see the world through the other person's eyes, empathy and caring will come naturally. Don't forget that laughter and humor are fun—

and sexy! Laughing with somebody is one of the most delightful experiences you can share.

- **Find things that you have in common with people and talk about them.** Don't forget that most folks are comfortable around people with whom they have something in common.

- **Find something that you really like about someone and share it with that person.** Remember, if you like someone, that individual will almost always like you back. If not, you don't need to be hanging around with that person, right?

- **Be approachable.** It's fine to maintain a level of mystery, but no matter how beautiful or how handsome you are, people will not approach you if you don't look happy, friendly, and receptive. In fact, stunningly good-looking people often have more trouble than average-looking people in this area because others automatically assume that beauty renders a person unreachable.

The first step, then, is to get out there and practice simply connecting with people. The next step is to overcome your resistance to actual flirting. While flirting may seem to come naturally to some people, it is a skill that anyone can learn.

So go ahead and try it. And yes, you have to practice. Just like playing tennis, riding a bike, or anything else, your flirting will improve with practice. The important thing is that you get out there and do it!

Now that you're feeling better about flirting let's explore the different varieties of flirtation.

Testing, Testing: One, Two…Wow!

Harmless flirting can be fun and ego-boosting.

As God Is My Witness, I Shall Never Flirt Destructively Again!

You can be pretty sure that those are words Scarlett O'Hara never said. We all remember the image of Scarlett seated so demurely at the center of a circle of fawning would-be suitors. With deft movements and subtle words, she held out to each of them the promise of her attentions, even her affections, if only they played their cards right.

In one scene of Gone With The Wind, she was flirting madly, leading the men on, enraging their women, and generally causing mayhem. Her intent was meaningless, beyond her desire to feel good about herself—everyone else's feelings are damned. The character of Scarlett was, in her fickleness, the epitome of the old-fashioned flirt—the destructive flirt, if you will.

What we so often forget is that Scarlett, as adept as she was at flirting and seduction, ended up alone and unhappy. Her very fickleness caused her to lose the one man she truly loved—and who truly loved her.

The old style of generally flirting had one very clear and very short-term objective: to attract someone's amorous attention. There was little or no thought given to the "next step," much less the final outcome of the actions. All that mattered was to get another person to notice and want you.

That's not to say that such an objective is inherently bad, of course. We all want to be noticed and desired. To some extent, we all wish to be seductive. It's in our wiring to want, even need, to attract the attention and affections of another human being. And flirting can be a fun and harmless means to gain attention.

Unfortunately, however, there are still many Scarletts (and their male counterparts) running around out there, flirting with disaster.

It happens all the time.

How do you avoid harmful flirting?

It's really just a matter of common sense and decency. If your intent is honorable, and you project those good intentions to those around you, you shouldn't run into any problems. And, since it is impossible to know for certain what a new acquaintance is thinking or, therefore, what his or her intentions are, you can only make sure your own motives are pure. Here are some pointers:

1. Ask yourself exactly what your flirtation is supposed to be saying to the another person? Do you promise just a bit of harmless and nonsexual fun, a night of steamy passion, a sizzling affair that lasts until you both get bored, or a possible lifetime together? Be careful what you're communicating.

2. Ask yourself if you are being truthful to the other person? Are you giving subtle hints that you might be willing to offer something you really aren't willing to give? You certainly don't want to find yourself in the uncomfortable position of having your actions "write checks that can't be cashed."

Perhaps you have the idea that the only way you'll make any headway is by offering the object of your desire what you think he or she wants. This may be as minuscule as a telephone call, as intimate as a sexual liaison, or as all-encompassing as an eventual trip to the altar.

Keep in mind, though, that there's just no way you can determine the needs of someone you've just met. You can, however, be sure of what you are willing to give and limit even your most subtle "promises" accordingly. You don't want to emit those confusing mixed signals we've all had to figure out at one time or another.

3. Don't flirt with somebody who is obviously with someone else. Sometimes this is hard to discern. We've all seen the married flirt who doesn't wear a ring and makes the rounds at parties, hitting on every attractive person in the room. But usually, you can tell who's with whom. If you have any doubt whatsoever, ask. If you're intimidated by such a direct approach, just play it safe and don't flirt with someone whose status you don't know.

4. If you're with somebody, don't flirt with anyone else.

Flirting as a prelude to passion

You've spotted someone whom you find particularly attractive, someone you want to get to know better. You aren't necessarily looking for a soul mate, but you wouldn't head for the hills if one appeared, either.

What you do want is the opportunity to get to know this person, spend some time together, and determine whether he or she is as attractive to you as you think.

It's time to turn on the charm.

This is where your literacy in nonverbal communication really comes into play (see Chapter 11). Many of the preliminary signals you send out during seductive flirting are the same as those used during harmless, equipment-check flirting (and, unfortunately, during destructive flirting too).

The difference, of course, lies in your intent and, if things go the way you've planned, in the results as well.

The Anatomy of seductive flirting

Truly seductive flirting is a synthesis of virtually everything we have talked about so far. It involves the approach techniques, the principles of connecting, and all the various forms of nonverbal communication we've discussed.

Seductive flirting is your unique expression of the sultry seductress or sexy seducer you have become. This is where you really begin to test those elements of seductiveness you've been developing.

When you're flirting seductively, you are flirting on several levels:

- Your physical self, through your general appearance, your body language, and your facial expressions.
- Your intellectual self, through your conversation.
- Your emotional self, through expressing empathy with the person you're trying to attract and through your attempts to get beyond this person's surface.
- Your essence, or spirit, which, as defined earlier, is at once a blend of the other ingredients and an element in and of itself. Your essence is reflected in your self-confidence, your sense of self-worth, and your intent.

Okay, maybe that's all sounding a little abstract, so let's get to some concrete stuff. Just how do you flirt seductively?

The sweetest sale you may ever make

If you've ever had any sales training, you probably learned various formulas for making a sale. The formula for seductive flirting is roughly the same, except, of course, the product you're selling is yourself, and the medium of exchange is a pleasure rather than money (well, I'm assuming).

Here is a simple formula that you can use as a guideline for your own seductive sale (see Chapters 10 and 11 for more information).

1. **Attention**: You can grab that attractive person's attention even from across the room if you just know the right signals. Smiling and judicious use of eye contact are great beginnings. Lip licking and playing with various props (your wine glass, your tie) can also be quite intriguing.

2. **Interest:** The process begins when someone first notices you, but it really hits its stride when you approach that person, or that person approaches you. Now you can use some of the up-close signals, such as whispering, leaning in, or tender touching. Presumably, verbal communication has begun, too—another powerful way of building interest.

3. **Desire:** Here's where you're beginning to make this person really want you. Turn up the heat a notch with a thigh touch or other mildly erotic gesture. Continue with the verbal communication, too, creating a sense of empathy with the person, and making the

object of your desire feel emotionally safe with you. (Make sure you feel emotionally safe, too, of course.)

4. **Conviction:** At some point, this person is going to become convinced he or she must find out more about you. Congratulations, you're almost there.

5. **Action:** Now you've really come to the point where something's gotta give. This is where you "close the deal"—you ask for a date, and the person accepts (or you are asked for a date, and you accept).

When you come right down to it, seductive flirting is really as simple as finding your prospect and selling your seductiveness to that individual. As for commissions and bonuses, well, that's entirely up to you and your partner!

Flirting, as we have seen, can be grievously misused. However, if you maintain your conscious commitment to the integrity of your own behavior, you will find that flirting can be a deliciously sensuous activity— a source of pleasure for both you and the person with whom you're flirting.

Done properly, it can provide a real boost to both your egos and get a new relationship off to an excellent start. So stamp that word "integrity" on the inside of your eyelids where you'll be constantly reminded, and get out there and have—them—a ball!

CHAPTER 10

The nine types of seducers

1. The Siren

The Siren is of highly charged traditionally feminine energy and tends to attract those of a completely opposite, traditionally-masculine energy. Whether or not you identify as male, female, or neither, you'll tend to be attracted to a Siren when you show characters on the extremes of traditionally-male behavior.

I absolutely hate using the words feminine and masculine because of the connotations behind each. When we think feminine, we think of the female sex, and when we think of masculine, we think of the male sex. However, feminine and masculine or just two ends of a behavioral spectrum, regardless of sex or gender.

Just know that from now on, do not envision a traditional-female figure when I say feminine/female, and do not envision a traditional-male figure when I say masculine/male. Whatever you identify as, you hold both male and female behaviors and energy.

For example, when you show rigidity, high responsibility, almost a coldness, and the need for control in things, the Siren is your opposite. The Siren plays on society's oppression of your inner desire for personal pleasure and play, most notably through your senses.

Think Cleopatra and Marilyn Monroe. These Sirens were attractive because of their ability to bring out a heightened masculine feeling in those they came in contact with.

Cleopatra brought exoticism and a sense of godly masculinity to both Julius Ceasar and Mark Antony (and probably many others), and Marilyn Monroe brought a sense of masculine danger and pleasure to Joe DiMaggio and John F Kennedy (and probably many others).

We're attracted to, and actively try to attract Sirens when we secretly just want to let go. When society needs us to be a strong rock, an emotionless stoic with many a responsibility, the Siren attracts us with the lure of opposing behavior we desperately long for.

Think back to your past crushes. Were you attracted to them because they made you feel extra masculine? Did they dangle a life of ease and little responsibility in your strict day-to-day affairs?

The trouble with Sirens is their ability to bring out laziness for short-term pleasure. To tackle and grow maturely with a Siren:

- Do not let your character suffer.
- Keep an open understanding of what you plan to do with your life.
- Never forget your life plan and do not let yourself be distracted for minimal pleasure.
- You have so much love to offer the world, do not stunt your talents.

2. The Rake

The Rake is characterized as the masculine Siren. Playing on society's roles that a female character must abide by, the Rake brings out the oppressed behaviors of a traditionally-feminine figure. They bring out the exciting feminine in us. Again, male, female, or neutral, we're attracted to

Rakes when we've been too confined and comfortable - too restrained - too neutral and unenergized in our day-to-day lives.

For example, when we've grown accustomed to the office banter, the politically correct and neutral acceptance of things, and our banal schedules, the Rake stirs things up and makes us feel special.

The Rake is guided by his enflamed passion for you at the expense of others and gives you the thrill of hot romance. Like the Siren, they strive to help you let go of responsibilities in favor of in-the-moment pleasure. No talk of future responsibilities.

Where the Siren attracts with visual sensuality, the Rake attracts with linguistic sensuality. The Rake is a master of language, communicative influence, and poetic verbiage.

Often, we may know we aren't going anywhere mature with a Rake, but that's what makes them so attractive. They are the heat of the moment and give us some texture in our dull lives. They could pull a casanova and hide in a closet until you're alone for the pleasurable taking.

Think Don Juan (or JGL's Don Jon), Christian Grey, or Chuck Bass from Gossip Girl. They'll say and do anything to get us to fall for them, and they're able to do so because we've been so bored.

Again, the majority of their attractiveness comes from their words, but it is the colorful and dangerous imagery they paint in our minds that becomes our daydreams.

The trouble with Rakes is their tendency to over-exaggerate their love and insinuate improbable fantasies of a lasting partnership.

To tackle and grow maturely with a Rake:

- Do not let your character suffer.
- Let them know of your life plans, and hold them accountable if they hold you back.
- Do not let yourself be hypnotized by their current words of pleasure. Keep track of their actions.
- You have so much love to offer the world, do not stunt your talents.

3. The Ideal Lover

The Ideal Lover comes to us from our childhood dreams, or rather our lost dreams. They are the ones that bring a hopeless fantasy to life with their ability to mirror the ideals we once had as innocent happy-go-lucky children but have lost to the grey world. They are highly astute at understanding our deepest desires and definitions of affection and bringing them to fruition.

Whatever it may be, the Ideal Lover takes the time to fully understand you and empathize with you. They play the long game. They study you and question you while giving you a sense of affectionate attention. And then they'll play your deepest desires to their advantage, accentuating the ideals you long for. They either show your desired ideals in themselves, or they try to make those ideals appear in you.

When this happens, we're hooked. We see a filling of a forgotten desire in them, with them, and through them. Often a chivalrous knight or a motherly damsel, or something completely different, they come to the rescue out of nowhere with a romanticized but real idea of love.

Think Casanova and John F Kennedy. Kennedy notably took the helm of a nation longing for lost ideals and future hope -- the epitome of the Ideal Lover. Tony Robbins does this with his clients, Gary Vaynerchuk with his entrepreneurial following, and Andy Warhol with his artistic subjects -- they were always painted in the most hopeful light.

The trick of the Ideal Lover is their ability to know what "hope" looks like to different people.

On the other hand, the trouble with Ideal Lovers is their grandiose self-image and lack of ability to operate within the realms of reality. Their high ideals are the culprit of this and, if left unchecked, can get too out of hand.

To tackle and grow maturely with an Ideal Lover:

- Allow for their hope and ideas of growth, but also keep a firm grounding in reality.
- Keep open communication for your life plans.
- Remember, they are only human and are not godlike myths - be cautious with their proposals and plans.
- You have so much love to offer the world, do not stunt your talents.

4. The Dandy

The Dandy is the Siren or the Rake of the same sex. They attract the traditionally male with psychologically masculine traits, and they attract the traditionally female with psychologically feminine traits. They tear down the labels that society has put on sexuality, and they play in all spaces.

121

We're attracted to Dandies for their ambiguous and obscure personas and their freedom to break prejudiced sexual behavioral roles.

Since humans are social creatures, our societies will always tend towards a general acceptance of values in order to keep everyone in place. Dandies defy this and let themselves explore multiple perspectives, especially those perspectives that are not accepted by society.

Often mysterious and unable to predict, Dandies spark our interest when we have repressed desires for freedom. Their lack of conformity to the masses is such an attractive characteristic that we all want a piece of. The fact that they easily flaunt it -- whether through their clothing, opinions, or overall behavior -- is something to be jealous of in itself. Why not try to obtain this freedom for ourselves?

Flamboyant males and rigid females are the popular images that come to mind. Think Rudolph Valentino and Lou Andreas-Salomé. The masculine Dandy and the feminine Dandy. They cast spells on the opposite gender using their same behaviors.

Valentino had a very feminine-described etiquette and appearance, and Salomé had very rigid independent habits. They attracted their lovers by showing how free they were to act like their lovers.

As progressive as these types sound, their strong ability to relate to you could also lead to trouble. Power struggles may be an issue since you'd most likely be sharing similar fields of work or goals. Another is the inevitable case of unconditional acceptance -- we come to expect them to understand us fully without even speaking, and this can only lead to miscommunication.

To tackle and grow maturely with a Dandy:

- Take inspiration from their free-spiritedness, but do not forget your responsibilities and the others you need.
- As you share similar fields of interest, do not deliberately try to outshine each other. It's not a competition.
- Do not let yourself be swayed by their indifference or unconcern for others. Always treat others respectfully.
- You have so much love to offer the world, do not stunt your talents.

5. The Natural

The Natural is a reflection of those golden years of comfort and innocent affection - childhood. They portray what both Kubrick and Freud would describe as 'uncanny.' Familiar yet strange. The Natural brings into their persona a sense of youthfulness in an adult body, drawing those that long for the times of no responsibilities, harmlessness, and naive spontaneity.

We miss those times, and the Natural brings them back to us. Their child-like mannerisms and kind of weakness are something that attracts us. They draw out sympathy in us through their subconscious actions of needing protection. They probably won't say it outright or explicitly ask you for motherly/fatherly-ness, but it's their openness for affection and protection that draws us so close.

They represent a world we've all left behind, and we see this as a doorway back to that playroom. The Natural mainly draws upon 4 characteristics that we have attracted to:

1. innocence,
2. blissful unawareness,

3. spontaneous talent/skill,

4. openness.

All 4 are key indicators of a Natural and can seem endearing to be around.

Think Charlie Chaplin, Paul McCartney, Lil Yachty, and Ryan Reynolds. They all emit this aura of youth that falls on us with an almost intoxicating feeling. Self-awareness and openness in their sincerity. They don't even try to act like the other adults.

While everyone hits us with seriousness and strict adulthood-ness, it's the Natural people that calm our senses and ease our anxieties of needing to be an overly cautious grownup.

Because if they can succeed this far as a child, why can't we?

The common obstacle while dealing with Naturals is their tendency to be too childish. Their innocence and naiveté can quickly turn into irritation as you start to feel too much like a parent. When you can't talk to them on an equal level and start to baby them, a sense of annoyance and irritability may start to arise.

To tackle and grow maturely with a Natural:

- Treat life with a light heart, but keep yourself aware of your responsibilities as growing individuals.
- Do not take the role of mother/father and child. Set your boundaries and expectations for one another.
- Find "adult things" to do and enjoy together. Don't rely on childhood memories to bring joy.
- You have so much love to offer the world, do not stunt your talents.

6. The Coquette

The Coquette is hot and cold.

They touch and go.

They attract you with hopeful words or sensual maneuvers and then step back and distance themselves from you. They entice you and frustrate you at the same time, and we're attracted to this because of our human nature to want what we can't have.

They tease us.

This may seem like an obvious unattractive trait, but the reason they spark any sort of infatuation is because of their ability to plant a seed of desire in our minds that continue to grow without them needing to be there. Consciously or subconsciously, they've come to understand what we desire and insinuate that they are the solution to our desires -- all without being present.

They are the ultimate tease because it is in their psychological enchantment that takes hold of our:

A) hoping for their surrender to us and,

B) the thought that we can be just as independent.

With the former, it is so common for both men and women to fawn over people they know they can't have or know they shouldn't have -- the grass is always greener on the other side.

With the latter, much like the Dandy, we want to be in the presence of someone just as carefree and unworried about the consequences of their actions -- and the Coquette does just that, showing little acknowledgment for us and giving hope that maybe we can have little worry for consequence as well.

Think Josephine de Beauharnais, John Mayer, Ginger from Casino, and every bachelor on The Bachelor. They dangle the love carrot on a stick in front of us but never fully give it to us. They use the virtue of delayed satisfaction to their advantage.

And this is exciting to us because we know how independent they are, but there's just that bit of hope that they could be dependent on us. And that satisfies both our human need to want what we can't have and our human need to feel significantly special.

Coquettes are like a shadow we cannot grasp but are always lingering behind us.

The apparent downside is their unreliability. They may show bouts of deep affection and loyalty to us (which gives us some of the biggest excitements and joys we can feel), but on the whole, they are difficult to tame and keep within our needs.

To tackle and grow maturely with a Coquette:

- Set the expectations right from the start. If you're willing to play hot and cold, let them know and let yourself know.
- Do not fall for their words or small acts of compassion -- keep a general tally of how reliable they act.
- Keep a firm grasp of your needs and never settle.

- You have so much love to offer the world, do not stunt your talents.

7. The Charmer

The Charmer has almost a devilish smile you're willing to swoon over. The word "charm" comes from the Latin "carmen" -- a song or a chant that is synonymous with a magic spell. To charm is to cast a spell on another. *The way that they do this, and the reasons we fall for them, is because they understand three fundamental laws of human nature:*

- the law of narcissism,
- the law of defensiveness,
- and the law of grandiosity.

It's our egos that they stroke, our emotional vanity walls that they align with, and our self-esteem that they praise.

Similar to the Ideal Lover, they make us feel special by playing on our deepest emotions and bringing them into warm light:

- ★ they make us feel like the center of attention,
- ★ bring us personalized pleasure,
- ★ diffuse any conflict,
- ★ relax us from chaos while keeping ourselves cool,
- ★ and have the skills/resources to help us in other areas of our lives.

They are the embodiment of a prince/princess charming.

Opposite the Ideal Lover, however, is that they actively try to repress any signs of sexuality or signs of overt romantic tension. They give us a bit of

127

Coquette-like distance and confusion in terms of romance while at the same time bringing Ideal Lover behavior.

This makes them seem extra valuable because we suspect that no others are able to hold them as we can. "Wow, he/she makes me feel so special, and he's a little shy too. I think I can own him/her as no one else can."

Think Drake, George Clooney, the Obamas, Joseph Gordon-Levitt, Jessica Alba, Amanda Seyfried, Leonardo DiCaprio, and Brad Pitt. Well put-together, witty and affectionate in their comments, obviously able to connect with higher-class individuals, and knows how to keep it G rated. The family man or woman show hints of tackling danger.

The obstacle with Charmers is in their ability to hide or subdue the less-clean history of their character. Everyone has their dark sides, and it's when we forget this that makes us susceptible to assuming their holiness. Sure, they can have an excellent track record, but understand that we are all human and have the ability to make mistakes.

To tackle and grow maturely with a Charmer:

- Set expectations for what you two are looking for. Don't expect they'll be able to love you unconditionally.
- Do not fully rely on them for your complete happiness - they can only give so much, and you need to keep self-reliance.
- Thoughts of being "too good to be true" could lead you to suspicion, but don't let this hinder your ability to love.
- <u>You have so much love to offer the world, do not stunt your talents.</u>

8. The Charismatic

The Charismatic is the excitement in the room. They exude confidence and energy in all the right places. They are mesmerizing, and we're attracted to them because of their sincere obsessions and opinions, and actions. They glow with a sense of charisma with their animated gestures and fiery persuasive voice. And if they fit our values, they're just a good time to be around.

They have a definite purpose in life and seem to spread their campaign in the most eloquent, magnetic, and theatrical way. It's hard not to be attracted to such people because they give us a sense of purpose through osmosis. If we lose sight of a meaningful life, it's their charismatic energy that makes us believe in ourselves once again. They are the light in the dark.

And with this, it is easy to be swayed and influenced by them. They have such a strong belief in themselves that it is hard to find flaws in their plans or their character. Similar to the Charmer of hope, the Charismatic brings intensified energy to their own hopes and tends to make you believe in them as well - which leads us to be more reliant and believe in their cause/values.

Think Gary Vaynerchuk, Grant Cardone, Will Smith, Al Pacino, Meryl Streep, Jennifer Lawrence, Robin Williams, and Jackie Chan. Their invigorating tone and influence get to you. Plus, they have a strong sense of awareness like the Charmer for cooling things down when need be.

There are a lot of entrepreneurial bloggers and YouTubers that praise charisma, and rightly so -- it does the job. But there are some obstacles that should be examined.

Such obstacles include their savior-like attitude and prophetic fervor. We're attracted to them at first because of this, but in the long term, this gallant behavior leads to fatigue. Psychologists call this 'erotic fatigue' when the feelings of passion are asking for too much of our energy and eventually lead to feelings of resentment.

Yes, too much love is exhausting. This leads us to irritability. It's our responsibility to control this.

To tackle and grow maturely with a Charismatic:

- Be open to their affectionate hope, but keep a firm grip on your own values.
- Understand that they are not superhumans and don't always have the right answers. Think carefully of their actions.
- Keep open communication when it comes to the amount of energy you need, you give, and that you must recharge.
- You have so much love to offer the world, do not stunt your talents.

9. The Star

The Star is almost (or completely is) a celebrity status. They like the Natural, pose the powers of the uncanny -- specifically mixing reality and myth. The star is a dream come true. Physically present, but almost legendary and mythic in essence. They are almost too dream-like to picture in front of us. We imagine them too far out of our league, and that is what makes them so attractive.

They have a strong reputation as something surreal and superior to our understanding of day-to-day life. They attract us with their Hollywood-esque aura but also with their down-to-earth ability to relate to us. They're up there with the stars but close enough to come in contact with us—not too out of our reach.

To most, having a crush on a star-like individual may seem natural and obvious. But digging deeper, we can attribute this attraction to our own seemingly boring, too natural, banal, and too real life. Like all the other archetypal lovers, we're attracted to them because we lack what they have. And they have out-of-this-world type lives. Or at least portray it.

Think of any celebrity. Any performing musician. Any touring author. Any interviewed actor/actress. They have attention and adventure plastered all over their perceived schedules, and we want that. Especially in this Instagram / YouTube / Facebook / Netflix / Snapchat era of showing off. When we see their following on social media, we want a piece of that for ourselves, and that's what makes them so attractive to our plain lives.

Although the Star may have a clean and bright reputation, your dynamic with them will also include some overlooked setbacks.

Like the Dandy, you may come to fight for attention.

Like the Charismatic, you may come to exhaustion with their affection.

Like the Coquette, you may feel frustrated with their independence.

I can only imagine how frustrating an actual celebrity's family must get when they're bombarded with the paparazzi (though it could also be invigorating from time to time).

We all have our crushes from the movies but think deeply about what it must be like being their partner.

To tackle and grow maturely with a Star:

- Come up with clear expectations for each other's needs for affection.
- Understand that you both still have your own dedicated circle of friends/family and accept each other's growth with others.
- Stay supportive of each other's goals, and remember that no one can bring support in the same way that you do for them.
- You have so much love to offer the world, do not stunt your talents.

CHAPTER 11

Types of women

Gender has been a prevalent theme for centuries, with the idea of femininity inferred to be the opposite of masculinity. Women are portrayed as fragile, innocent creatures who use their "feminine wiles" to ensnare men.

But there is more than one type of woman, and they come in many flavours. With this book, I hope to illuminate the complex relationships between gender and sexuality by breaking down female seduction into three types:

1. good girls,
2. bad girls,
3. and queens (or however you like).

Each seductress enters into her profession with different intentions and motivations. While the process of seduction is similar among each type, their unique approach to the art of seduction leaves a lasting impression on their target.

The Good Girl

The good girl's objective is to become a *"woman that every man dreams about but knows he can never have."* She will never fall for a man who isn't her knight in shining armor and focuses on men who are already engaged or already married. Her fantasy love story is "Romeo and Juliet," with herself as Juliet and her target as Romeo.

She never tells her partners about her true feelings for them because she believes love comes from within. Instead, she focuses on showing her partner why she loves him through her willingness to do his laundry, cook for him, and clean their house.

She shows her partner that she is a good girl through emotional labor and devotion to his needs. Her target usually never realizes that he is being seduced by her good-girl act because he believes they are in a genuine relationship.

The Bad Girl

The bad girl relies primarily on physical appearance and sexual availability to attract men.

She is very confident in herself and is not afraid to show it off as much as possible. She wants men to be physically attracted by her appearance without even knowing who she really is.

Sometimes, she will even make up derogatory things about her target as a way of putting him at ease. She is also very sexual and uses small intimate conversations to get information about the man's sexual fantasies and desires.

The Bad Girl's personality and approach to seduction are usually not recognized by her targets, because they are very good at pretending to be a bad girl who is "easy" and "down-to-earth" just to get what they want. However, some men do realize that their connection might not be as genuine as they thought it was in the beginning. This is why the bad girl type has a tendency to move from man to man.

The Queen

The Queen's approach is characterized by her "sophistication, elegance and high self-esteem." She understands how men think and how much better she knows men than they know themselves.

Her interest in seduction comes from her desire to be loved and desired for who she really is and not for who others want her to be. She knows her worth, doesn't need validation, and takes full ownership of herself.

The queen looks at the world with a keen eye, breaking down every layer until she gets to the truth of an individual or an object. She enjoys the notion of having nothing to prove to others, specifically her target.

She takes pleasure in knowing that all she needs is herself to succeed and that she "is completely her own woman."

The Queen typically won't have a problem getting what she wants from her targets because of the power that comes with choosing for yourself.

This type of female seduction has one main objective: total liberation through true self-love and empowerment.

The queen lives by the mantra of "Take what you want, but ask for more in return" — this way, she knows that what she has is hers to give out and not hers to keep. The beauty of the queen lies in her ability to get what she wants while also giving it to others.

A good girl uses her target's respect to gain access to his dreams and desires, while the bad girl aims for his sexual organs. The queen knows how highly her target values himself, so she sets herself up as a challenge that he cannot refuse.

Her approach directly contradicts all of the other types because she won't give him what he wants but rather helps him discover that it is within himself to be what he wants: powerful, fierce, and completely deserving of love.

The genuine nature of the queen's seduction leads to her being seen as a real woman instead of the bad girl or good girl who disguises themselves as one. While she obviously knows what she wants, she does not pretend to be anything that she is not.

Her goal is to be loved, respected, and understood.

The queen has control of herself and her body and will not let anyone use her for their own sexual pleasure without giving something back in return. She doesn't care about the superficial things that the other types care about: clothes, status, and money. She has elevated herself far beyond these things by learning how to take what she wants using her mind, body, and soul.

Women who uses their seduction as a means to an end are considered bad girls because they use their targets to get what they want without any consideration for them. Women like them have an air of entitlement and are often in desperate need of emotional attention.

Good girls focus on giving their partners what they want and often sacrifice themselves for their partners' emotional needs.

The Queen focuses on herself, making herself the priority in her relationship with others and not being used by another person.

The Queen tends to move from one man to another because she doesn't believe in committing long-term relationships. She knows that she is worth more than that and is independent enough to choose her company based on her own desires and personal interests.

If she is in a relationship, she will not give up her freedom to please another person and will always need to know that the relationship is about her.

The Bad Girl has no issue with leaving a relationship if it does not get what she wants in return for her sexual services. She has no respect for others and cares less about them as human beings. The Bad girl's approach to seduction is based purely on physical appearance, brashness, and sexual availability.

People who are attracted by this type of woman usually aren't looking for love or commitment, so they can be much easier targets for exploitation. The Bad Girl lives in the fast lane and doesn't worry about tomorrow.

The Good Girl is an emotional manipulator. She cares about others more than herself and will put their needs ahead of her own. She will support anyone who is sad, lonely, or feeling down because that is what she wants others to do for her when she feels the same way.

The Good Girl can not perform self-care because she puts everyone else's needs before her own, which makes it hard for her to be true to herself because she constantly worries about how others will react if they find out how fake she really is.

The Queen takes seduction very seriously and uses it as a way to express herself. She has no problem with being alone because she knows that relationships are temporary. The Queen is not afraid to be alone because she knows that, in order for her to truly love another person, she must first love herself.

The Queen knows how fragile relationships can be and how easily they can fail. Instead of wasting her time trying to make something last when she knows it won't, she focuses on empowering others so that they do not waste their time on things that will never last.

The Queen is the female equivalent of the "alpha male." She does not know the meaning of "fear" and is able to achieve anything she desires.

CHAPTER 12

How to apply self-confidence and self esteem to the female seduction arts

In the world of self-confidence, there are both genders. Women have their share of struggles with self-confidence, and society places many expectations on a woman to have confidence in herself.

Why is this?

But why do women struggle with self-confidence? What is the connection between confidence and well-being for women? And how can they overcome these obstacles to start embracing themselves again?

This book will explore these questions, looking at what it means to be confident and how women can cultivate a more confident mindset.

You will find your inner peace again and learn that you are equal to anyone else out there.

Generally, being confident is an inner sense of knowing that we are doing well and have the ability to handle any situation. This plays into a positive mental attitude, which can be defined as: *"a positive and healthy state of mind that allows users to believe in themselves and be at ease with obstacles or challenges.*

From this definition, you can get a better understanding of what it means to have self-confidence.

In addition, remind yourself that confidence is a feeling of security in your capabilities. It can be as simple as telling yourself, "I am able to do this," or "I am capable of making something happen.

As we discussed, there are both positive and negative perceptions of self-confidence. Negative self-confidence could be described as being overconfident or "excessive" belief in one's own abilities. As defined here, people who are overconfident may lack true appreciation for themselves and their actions. This can lead to poor decision-making and failure to recognize a situation for what it really is.

In contrast, "realistic confidence" could be described as the true sense of confidence that someone has in their abilities. In addition, realistic confidence does not mean arrogance or disrespect. People with realistic confidence understand themselves and can make rational decisions about a situation.

Let's take a look at how we can cultivate realistic confidence in ourselves.

Self-respect is very important in feeling confident about oneself and what you can do for the world around you. In addition, respect for others is an indication of respect for yourself.

If someone does not have respect for those around them, it could be a sign that they are struggling with their self-confidence and need to check themselves before making rash decisions or stepping on other people's toes (literally or figuratively). This can have negative effects on one's relationships with others, friends, and family.

It is also important to know what you are good at as a person. Take the time to analyze your accomplishments, both big and small. This is a great way to strengthen your realistic confidence in your abilities. It builds on the fact that you are a person with value and can contribute something meaningful to society.

If you have been able to make it this far in life so far, then you are doing something right! Be proud of yourself for all that you have done and all of your accomplishments. If there is something that is keeping you down or preventing you from achieving your goals, then take the necessary steps to change it or remove yourself from those negative situations.

Women who exhibit realistic confidence in themselves should be lauded as they are people who can achieve great things and stand out among others. They work to make the world a better place and support others in their endeavors.

Being confident can be a great way to bring out your inner charisma and bring out your best qualities. By taking the time to analyze yourself and understand what you are capable of doing, you can start to tap into your self-confidence and use it as a tool for success in your life.

CONCLUSION

No book about seduction would be complete without talking about love.

After all, for the majority of us, sex is most fulfilling in the context of a loving relationship—and most people, at some point, do fall in love.

No doubt, many of you who are reading this book are in the process of falling in love, are already in love, or simply have a future goal of finding the Big L but aren't quite there yet. Perhaps you're even already in a committed relationship.

That's why I'm going to devote this chapter to take a closer look at this phenomenon we call love. While it is beyond the scope of this book to delve into the details of compatibility and commitment, I will share some insights about love: the different kinds of love and the phases of a love relationship.

And because I haven't forgotten why you came to this book in the first place—the role that seduction plays as the relationship progresses. And I'll end the chapter—and the book—by talking about how you can make seduction last forever.

When love is on the agenda (whether you planned it or not)

Men's and women's roles are changing as we approach the new millennium. Many of you guys are becoming more relationship-oriented, and many of you women are becoming more independent.

142

It's no longer true, if it ever was, that men are just out for "one thing" (sex) and that women are interested only in marriage. Even so, it is true that many people enter into the process of seduction with agendas that would seem to be more consistent with traditional sex roles:

- To some men, seduction is simply a means to get a woman into bed.
- To some women, seduction is a means of getting a man to fall in love and propose marriage.

Obviously, there is enormous potential for trouble if either one of these agendas clashes with the partner's plans for the relationship. In a perfect world, both parties would have no agenda other than to enrich each other's lives with the experience.

They would be open to whatever happened without being unduly attached to the outcome. In reality, most people are rarely that detached. At the very least, partners should have compatible expectations for the relationship.

Sometimes, however, expectations change. One or the other partner in the couple who was in it only for the sex may find him or herself falling in love. The partner who is marriage-minded may decide he or she would rather wait a while longer before jumping into such a serious commitment.

No matter how careful we are and how well we think we know ourselves or our partners, the human heart is often unpredictable. Lust is bewildering enough, but when love enters into the picture too, it can really throw us for a loop.

So what do you do when love calls you by your name, as the old Leonard Cohen song puts it? For that matter, how do you know it's really love calling, as opposed to infatuation? Let's start by exploring what love is.

Just what the heck is true love, anyway?

Love is an emotion that nearly everyone has experienced at some time in his or her life. You would think, then, that we'd all be able to agree on what it is.

But this hasn't been the case.

After all, there are different kinds of love. Furthermore, the experience of love is different for everybody. There are as many definitions of true love as there are people to define it.

For centuries, philosophers, poets, and novelists have tried to capture it in words, and artists and sculptors have attempted to capture it in forms and images. In more recent decades, social scientists and biologists have tried various ways to quantify it.

So far, there's no real consensus about what real love is. The only point on which we all seem to agree is that it exists.

It should come as no surprise that I don't have the ultimate definition of love, either.

But I will offer you the best indicator I know of the presence of real love: It is when you put the other person's needs on an equal basis with your own—not below them (that's selfishness), nor above (that's martyrdom).

As many of you have probably already learned the hard way, the road to real love is often rocky. How do you know when you're on that road, and what can you do to keep love alive and exciting once you've reached your destination? We can begin solving this mystery by taking a look at how a romantic relationship develops.

Love never remains static

One thing most of us can agree on is that love never remains in a static condition. The love between two people grows and changes, like the people themselves. It either gets better or fades, but it never stays the same. Even though the experience of love is different for everybody, however, most romantic relationships go through fairly predictable stages:

- passionate love
- and mature love.

In the beginning: passionate love

Some call it infatuation, some call it insanity, but most of us agree that it's glorious. I'm talking, of course, about that fevered state known as passionate love. Passionate love is a state of fierce longing for your partner.

At this early stage in your romantic relationship, the two of you are completely absorbed in each other, and it's often difficult to tell where lust ends, and love begins. Perhaps that point is moot—unless, of course, you're thinking of making a long-term commitment when you're still at this stage.

You should not make any crucial life decisions while under the influence of passionate love. That's because, during this time of wondrous highs (and devastating lows when things don't go right), the two of you really are not in your right minds.

Let's face it: Passionate love makes most of us a little crazy— in a good way, but crazy nonetheless. And, much as we may wish it, that delicious high doesn't last. Eventually, the endorphin levels drop off, and things get more or less back to normal. We're simply not wired for perpetual ecstasy.

Of course, this doesn't stop some people from trying to maintain a state of constant rapture. Since it's almost impossible to sustain a passionate high with one person, people who are hooked on that new love feeling will go from partner to partner, ending the relationship as soon as the newness wears off.

These "love addicts" may leave the proverbial trail of broken hearts behind them, but in the end, they're the ones who suffer the biggest heartbreak.

For those who stick it out past the infatuation stage, what comes next?

Is it all boredom and stagnation from there on out?

Unfortunately, this is true for some couples. However, in the best-case, people who continue to nurture their relationships can reap the rewards of a deeper kind of love.

As time goes by, mature love

No matter how hot and passionate love is, eventually and inevitably, it simmers down. For most couples, the passion begins fading within two to four years. People have different ways of coping with this loss of "paradise," but there are certain discernible patterns.

Studies have shown, for example, that couples don't express affection to each other as frequently after about two years. Furthermore, in cultures worldwide, the divorce rate peaks after about four years of marriage.

What gives?

As mentioned previously, the fading of passionate love is partly a biochemical phenomenon where endorphin production returns to normal levels with the passage of time.

Then there's the emotional reality of getting to know somebody. Any illusions you may have had at the beginning about your partner's perfection are inevitably replaced with the day-to-day actuality of being with someone who is, after all, only human—just like you.

The result of reality setting in that the highs in the relationship isn't as high. The good news is that the lows aren't as low either, but that may be small comfort for those who are hooked on the thrill.

If love is to last, it must settle into a steadier but still warm state known variously as mature love or companionate love. This type of love is characterized by true bonding and emotional intimacy. Other factors besides physical attraction, such as shared values and shared experiences, become increasingly important.

And while love in its more mature stages may be more low-key than passionate love, it is deeper and, some would say, in many ways, it is sweeter.

The important thing to know is that companionate love does not preclude passion. It's not a complete trade-off, where you give up passion and get endurance in exchange. You may have to work harder at keeping the passion alive, but you can keep it alive for as long as you both wish.

As a matter of fact, I believe that a lasting relationship must include passion in order to be truly satisfying. The other two components of a successful long-term relationship are compatibility and commitment.

So...Where does seduction fit into this?

If we're to accept the idea that seduction is a never-ending process, we need to be aware of how it fits into our lives as the relationship grows and changes. Let's take a closer look at the role seduction plays in the different phases of a romantic relationship.

- **Infatuation phase.** In this phase seduction plays the most obvious part—the starring role if you will. At the beginning of your relationship, everything is new and enchanting. There is magic in the air around you. You're in the throes of passionate love, and virtually everything about your relationship is seductive. Seduction is what makes you both keep coming back for more.

- **Middle phase.** At this point, some of the newnesses are wearing off, but seduction continues to play a pretty strong part. It just requires a little prodding once the initial excitement wanes. This is why it is so important that you continue to seduce each other on all levels and that you create adventures together so your relationship doesn't become stagnant.

- **Decision/commitment phase.** Sooner or later, if your love lasts long enough, and you are both so inclined, you will reach a point where you're considering taking your relationship to the next level. For some couples, this means moving in together, for others, it means marriage. In any case, when you are making a decision to commit to someone, seduction should not play a major role. This doesn't mean you suspend seduction and passion altogether. Still, for a major decision such as commitment, you need to let your head and your heart be your guide rather than your libido. That's why it's extremely important that you don't attempt to make any long-term commitments while you are still in that wild- and-crazy infatuation stage.

- **Postcommitment phase.** Now is the time for you to haul seduction out from wherever you temporarily placed it while you were making your big decision to commit to each other. Once you've made your commitment, seduction is not only desirable, and it is necessary to keep the passion alive. Many people think that after the initial passion fades—an average of two to four years into the relationship—this is the beginning of the end of passion. That is emphatically not true. You can make the passion last indefinitely. This may take some work, but the rewards are worth it.

Can we talk about commitment?

What if it looks as if your love is going to be much more than just another "affair to remember"?

What if you want it to be "an affair to continue"?

What if you're thinking about that "C" word: commitment?

Well, first of all, I don't believe you can, or should, make a commitment to somebody until you have been with that person long enough to determine whether, you are truly compatible.

Commitment means different things to different people. Or rather, different people express their commitment in different ways. For most people in our society, marriage is the ultimate expression of commitment. Unfortunately, it is possible to be married and not committed.

The act of getting married is, after all, an outward expression of intent. If, however, it is not backed up by true commitment—an internal pledge both partners must make in their hearts—it will be nothing more than an act.

You cannot force anybody to commit to you.

So, no matter how passionately in love (and in lust) you are, there are two principles to remember when you're trying to make up your mind about commitment:

1. Take your time. I recommend not making a decision until you've been together for at least a year.
2. Use your head. Passion and seduction play significant roles in getting the relationship underway and in keeping it intriguing over the long haul. But they should not be the major factors in making the all-important decision to commit to somebody.

Seduction can be forever—make it so!

If I didn't believe that seduction can be forever, I wouldn't have devoted an entire book to this topic. I hope by now you're convinced that seduction is a process and that it's up to you to choose how long that process.

Of course, there's only one first time with your partner, but that doesn't mean that the two of you can't continue to discover thrilling new things about each other—and yourselves and the world around you—for as long as your relationship lasts.

So how do you make seduction last forever?

You do it by making conscious choices about the relationship and yourselves. As you'll see, these choices reinforce each other.

Choose to stay in love with the relationship

For a relationship to continue to be fulfilling, you need to continue to focus on its positive traits. Too often, relationships begin a slow (or fast) decline once the passion wears off. Eventually, not only is the passion gone, but so is the love.

In most cases, this is because the partners have forgotten to focus on what worked in the relationship. It has somehow become easier for them to concentrate on what's not working. If you find this happening to you, you both need to go back to Chapter 1 and rediscover the magic that first drew you to each other.

One way to do this is to keep doing romantic and fun things together (or start doing them again if you've quit). Suppose the relationship is to survive, both of you must continue to associate it with good times. Some psychologists call this the "liking by association" principle. Whatever you call it, it works.

Choose to keep seducing your partner

To stay in love with the relationship and keep the passion alive, you need to continue to seduce your partner on all levels. Of course, you must be motivated to do this, and in order to be so motivated, you have to continue to focus on your partner's positive traits.

This can sometimes be a challenge in long-term relationships. It's inevitable that intimate partners are going to find fault with each other sooner or later. When faultfinding becomes a habit, however, you need to take a few steps back and remember why you were so attracted to your lover in the first place. And then you need to choose to keep seducing that attractive person.

Choose to keep seducing yourself

In order to be able to focus on the positive traits in your partner, you must also continue to focus on the positive traits in you. In other words, you have to keep seducing yourself.

How do you do this?

First, you take care of yourself:

- physically,
- intellectually,
- emotionally,
- and spiritually.

Continue your personal growth—and never stop growing.

Change is a characteristic of life, and since you're going to change anyway, for better or worse, why not make it for better? Go back to the beginning of this book as often as you need to. Do the exercises that focus on developing your seductiveness on all levels. Continue to be seduced by life, and you, in turn, will continue to be seductive—to yourself and your partner.

It's inevitable.

Let Love and Seduction feed on each other

When you think about it, love and seduction are natural partners. And if you can remain in love with yourself, your partner, the relationship, and life, there's no reason you can't make seduction last forever—or, as they sometimes say these days in wedding vows: for as long as you both shall live.

Printed in Great Britain
by Amazon

23539893R00086